# JUDAS AND JESUS

Also by Jean-Yves Leloup

*The Gospel of Mary Magdalene*

*The Gospel of Philip:*
*Jesus, Mary Magdalene, and the Gnosis of Sacred Union*

*The Gospel of Thomas:*
*The Gnostic Wisdom of Jesus*

*The Sacred Embrace of Jesus and Mary:*
*The Sexual Mystery at the Heart of the Christian Tradition*

# JUDAS AND JESUS

## *Two Faces of a Single Revelation*

Jean-Yves Leloup

Translated by Joseph Rowe

Inner Traditions
Rochester, Vermont

Inner Traditions
One Park Street
Rochester, Vermont 05767
www.InnerTraditions.com



Originally published in French under the title *Un homme trahi: Le roman de Judas* by Albin Michel, Paris
First U.S. edition published in 2007 by Inner Traditions



**Library of Congress Cataloging-in-Publication Data**
Leloup, Jean-Yves.
[Homme trahi. English]
Judas and Jesus : two faces of a single revelation / Jean-Yves Leloup ; translated by Joseph Rowe. — 1st U.S. ed.
p. cm.
Includes bibliographical references and index.
ISBN-13: 978-1-59477-166-8 (pbk.)
ISBN-10: 1-59477-166-9 (pbk.)
1. Judas Iscariot. 2. Jesus Christ. I. Title.

BS2460.J8L4513 2007
226'.092—dc22

2006030467

Printed and bound in Canada by Webcom

10 9 8 7 6 5 4 3 2 1

Text design and layout by Rachel Goldenberg
This book was typeset in Adobe Caslon with Centaur as the display typeface

*To Michelle de Broca*

*To Patrick and Natasha Alessandrin*

*It's time to get started,*

*and do what Christianity has never done:*

*take care of the damned.*

ALBERT CAMUS

# *Contents*

# *Publisher's Note to the Reader*

Readers familiar with the books by Jean-Yves Leloup will note that, unlike his earlier titles published by Inner Traditions, in this book he has adopted a narrative reconstruction technique to describe the life of Judas and his relationship with Jesus. The text is based on both the canonical and the apocryphal sources (with an emphasis on the canonical), including the recently discovered Gospel of Judas. In his analysis of this relationship, the author examines the mystic unity that lies behind the dualist roles the two men played.

In trying to discover the real Judas, the author asks himself: "Why must we always treat history and myth as if they were adversaries?" He notes that often legends become so powerful that the historical figure falls into the shadows. Leloup has re-created the life of Judas using illustrative dialogue that evokes the early Christian faith and, in so doing, beautifully and evocatively discovers the deep and everlasting relationship between Judas and Jesus.

# I

# *Childhood*

Judas was eight years old when the other children first threw stones at him. One of them yelled: "Why are you so ugly, Judas, and so ill-tempered? Is it your parents' fault, or your own?" Judas fled, more to hide his tears than to escape the stones.

Who indeed had brought him into the world in this way? And why—by what design—was he so ugly and so violent already? Above all, why was he so unhappy?

Someone had to be guilty. Rather than examining himself and trying to reconstruct an ancestral past that escaped him, Judas preferred to blame his parents. And in this, no righteous Jew would have contradicted him. His family was widely regarded with disgust. They were close to Herod, the bloody usurper and Roman collaborator who had recently died. There was a saying: "Herod sneaked onto the throne like a fox, ruled like a tiger, and died like a dog."

Yet it was this same Herod the Great who had rebuilt the Temple of Jerusalem in all its splendor, harking back to the time of Solomon. It was clear, however, that his own glory interested him more than the glory of God. With age, his character only worsened—having killed all his political rivals, he turned his attentions to his own family. His two eldest sons, Alexander and Aristobulus, were strangled, along with three hundred of their supporters. Two days before his death, he had his son Antipater arrested and killed. It was also said that he had ordered many children killed because one of them might be the Messiah.

Judas remembered nothing of the day of that massacre, but when a close friend of his father's told him the story, he began to vomit from the shame and horror of it. How could innocent children be killed in this way? If the Messiah was alive, he must surely feel guilty, knowing that his birth was the occasion for such a bloodbath. How could Jews, men of his own blood and of the high aristocracy, commit an atrocity that so blatantly violated Moses' sacred commandment written in the Torah, *Thou shalt not kill*? And how could YHWH allow the birth of his Messenger to give rise to such a massacre of innocents? Could the birth of this most beautiful and long-awaited child ever justify such an intolerable crime?

Very early, Judas began to feel himself a stranger to his family. The bonds of blood seemed too binding and too bloody.

It was said that he was conceived at the palace during one of the nights of orgy in which his mother often participated. Ruben Simon had acknowledged him as his son, though no one could be certain of it, and in any case he did not resemble his father. In fact, he looked like no one else in his family (some malicious gossips even wondered if it was with a human being that his mother had fornicated on that night).

As soon as he learned to read, he found his solace in the sacred scriptures. His favorite was the Book of Job. He felt close to Job and, like him, began to curse the day he was born:

> Let the day perish when I was born, and the night in which it was said, a male child has been conceived!

Let that day be darkness; let God not notice it from above,
neither let the light shine upon it.
Let darkness and the shadow of death obliterate that day; let a
cloud cover it; let an eclipse fall upon it.
As for that night, let darkness seize it; let it not be counted in
the days of the year, let it be absent from the number of the
months.
Lo, let that night be solitary, let no joyful voice come into it.
May those who curse the day curse it, prepared even to awaken
Leviathan!
Let the stars of that dawn go out; let that day look for light, but
find none; neither let it see any dawn.
Because it failed to shut the doors of my mother's womb, failed
to hide this sorrow from my eyes.
Why did I not die in the womb? Why did I not give up the
ghost as soon as I emerged from it?
Why was there a lap to receive me? Why were there breasts to
feed me?
Now I could be lying in peace, sleeping the peace of death,
Along with kings and counselors of the world, who built deso-
late tombs for themselves,
Or with princes who filled their tombs with gold and silver:
I would rather have been a secret abortion, not existing, like
those who never see the light of day.*

Judas was surprised to find a seeming defense of abortion in a sacred text, but how deeply he resonated with it! What good was there in being born, only to be subjected to the contempt of those near him and the rejection of those whom he would have liked to love—to say nothing of living in a body he would never have chosen?

---

*Job 3:3–16.

"Better to have been one of those innocent infants massacred by Herod. At least then my memory would be linked with that of the Messiah, who had just been born."

As had been predicted from Rome to Jerusalem, the death of Herod the Great plunged Judaea into chaos. Archelaos and Antipas, the two potential successors, hastened to Rome, where the emperor Augustus himself took upon the task of arranging the succession. Archelaos, though the elder, had a Samaritan mother. He received only half the kingdom of his father and the title of ethnarch of Judaea and Samaria, while Antipas received the title of tetrarch of Galilee and Perea. By thus calming the animosity between these two brothers, Augustus hoped to gain more control over groups who were resisting Roman occupation, especially the Zealots.

Judas was brought up by servants appointed to the task, his parents having neither the time nor the inclination to devote themselves to him. This left him often alone and absorbed in strange daydreams. Others might think him ugly, but he was certain that his soul was beautiful and noble, of a royal lineage very different from that of the Herod. The Pharisees, Essenes, and other pious followers of the Law might call him impure because of his family's moral reputation as well as their links with the occupiers, but he was certain of the righteousness of his intentions. His soul was thirsty and starving, filled with a sense of injustice, and he began to feel he had received a call to work for the reign of God.

When he was twelve, he was taken to Jerusalem and, because of his parents' standing, allowed to enter the Temple. In the hall where animals were butchered and burned for sacrifice, he was overcome by the odor of blood and burning flesh. As he fell into a faint, these words of scripture came to him, as if an echo of his own prayer:

"Adonai, You accept neither sacrifices nor offerings. But You have made this body for me, so I say: Here I am, I come to You my Lord, to do Your will."

When he regained consciousness, he wondered about the implications: If God does not accept burnt offerings, should Judas sacrifice his body to accomplish God's will? Why should the Messiah give his life to liberate his people from slavery and death? The truth was that Judas was not very attached to his own life. What he was looking for was an opportunity to rid himself of his bad blood and don a body of light. In this way, he would prove that his ugliness was not a punishment from God, for it would enable him to mingle with the poor and despised and help to prepare them for the great revolt against injustice, against the ongoing blasphemy of the occupation of the Holy Land by infidels.

God must be avenged, and obliged to fulfill his promises.

It was among the Zealots that he found a sympathetic echo of the thoughts and feelings that tormented his soul. These were the people of zeal, of ardent devotion to God and to the Torah. Sometimes they were known as the Sicarii, from *sica,* the name of the small dagger that they always carried so as never to forget that there was such a thing as just violence and just war for the honor of God, his land, and his chosen people. And now that land, people, and promise were being trampled or thrown into doubt.

It was not long before the Zealots became his new family—his true family, for it was he who had chosen them. How can the bonds of blood be compared to the bonds of spirit?

# 2

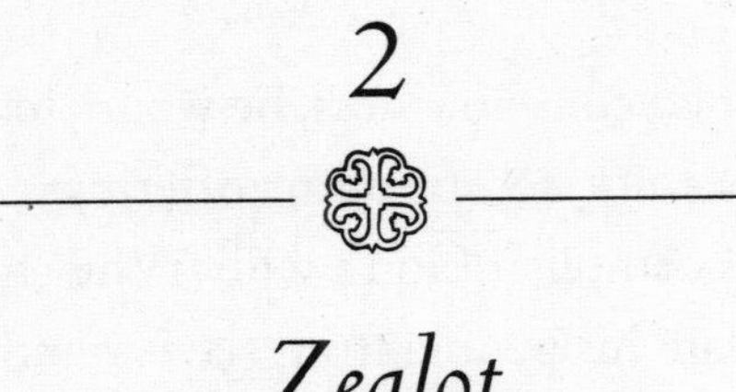

# *Zealot*

In spite of the fact that his father, Ruben Simon, had named him in a spirit of derision, Judas loved his name—Yehuda in Hebrew. It was the name of the fourth son of Jacob and Leah, spoken of in Genesis 29:35:

> And she conceived again, and bore a son, and she said: This time I will praise YHWH. Therefore she gave him the name Judah, and he was her last child.

He loved the five consonants of the name Y-H-W-D-H, in which the consonants of the divine Name are embedded: the tetragrammaton YHWH. Furthermore, the letters HWDH mean "praise." Hence Judah, or Judas, was the leader of the tribe whose mission is to praise YHWH. It was fitting that Judah was Leah's last child, for it signifies the ultimate reason for Israel's existence: to witness and render homage to the Eternal One. Judas felt that his name was his mission as well. With this ill-favored body, face, and family he would praise "the One who Is What He Is" and destroy everything that opposed this righteous praise, this orthodox way.*

There was another name that pleased him, which also contained the sacred tetragrammaton within it: the name Yeshua (Aramaic for "Jesus"; Yehoshua in Hebrew†). Its meaning was "God [YHWH] is Savior, Liberator." In his fantasies of saving his people, he had sometimes thought this name would have fit him even better. He desired to see himself either as the Messiah or, at least, as a companion of the Messiah of Israel.

At this point, Judas could not really see himself as a possible Messiah for his tribe, the Judaeans. Yet he was sometimes troubled when he read the books of the prophets, such as Isaiah 53:2–5, which speaks of the coming of a Messiah who would draw down upon himself the scorn of the very people he had come to save. Sometimes it seemed that every word was written for him:

> For he grew up before him like a young plant, and like a root out of dry ground; he had no form that attracted us to look at him, and no beauty that we should be pleased by him.
>
> He was despised and rejected by men; a man of sorrows, and acquainted with grief; and he was despised as one from whom men turn their faces, and we esteemed him not.
>
> Surely he has borne our grief and carried our sorrows; yet we judged him ill-favored, smitten by God, and afflicted.
>
> But he was wounded for our transgressions, he was bruised for our iniquities; upon him was the chastisement that made us whole, and with his wounds we are healed.

If it was not Judas himself the prophet was describing, it was at any rate a Messiah whom Judas ardently desired to serve.

---

*In Greek, *orthos* means "straight" and *doxa* means "praise."

†[The name Yehoshua was often shortened, particularly by Aramaic-speaking Jews, to Yeshua.]

Judas came to feel close to another Judas, known as the Galilean, son of the famous Hezekiah, who rebelled against the Romans and against Herod's power. Herod had the father killed, and after the king's death, Hezekiah's son Judas took up the torch and managed to acquire many arms with the help of allies. They also financed his plans for armed resistance.

When the Roman procurator Quirinias ordered a new census to ensure that no one escaped Caesar's taxes, the Jews of Jerusalem were divided. The high priest Joazar advised obeying the Roman order. But Judas the Galilean, supported by the Pharisee Sadoq, urged the people to resist. It was widely whispered by them that it was a great dishonor to consent to pay tribute to the Romans, thereby acknowledging a mortal master, when their only master was God.

From this moment on, Judas the Galilean became the leader of a veritable army, growing in numbers. They took refuge on the high plateaus and commanded reliable relay posts linking them to Jerusalem. It was in one of these posts that the two men called Judas finally met. Along with their name, they found they had the same aspiration: to be rid of the Herods and the Roman occupiers as soon as possible. By faith and by force they would drive these demons out of the Holy Land.

The Zealots found support among a people groaning under the burden of taxes as well as among many Pharisees, who shared their passion for strict obedience to the Law of the Torah, though they did not approve of the Zealots' violent methods.

The Sadducees and the Levites were regarded by the Zealots as enemies of God and his people. These were the great priestly families who had grown rich from Temple revenues and collaboration with Rome. They were more tolerant of the Essenes, who had also broken with the Temple establishment. Living in desert retreats, the

Essenes hoped that through prayer and a pure life they would hasten the coming of the Teacher of Righteousness, whom they regarded as at least a precursor to the Messiah.

For Judas, it was clear that the Messiah foretold by the prophets must also be the true King of the Jews long awaited by the people. He would not be of the lineage of the Herods, who were only half Jews, in any case, and behaved like heathens. This title could be borne only by a man of pure lineage and impeccable life, for it was the most noble of titles, even higher than that of Cohen (priest) or Nabi (prophet). Yet Judas was well aware that the Romans had forbidden this royal title and that anyone who presented himself as the King of the Jews would quickly be crucified, like those who had already claimed themselves kings and met this fate, false though their claims were.

During this time, Judaea was infested with bands of robbers, and it seemed that every time a group of these malcontents gathered, they elected a king. This led only to more misery for the Jewish people—for the Romans, the Jews were no more than a minor trouble to be dealt with harshly, but for the people as a whole, they were "the scourge which advances deeper into the darkness."*

Judas had a vivid memory of Simon of Transjordan, a highly placed administrator of Herod. He had been a handsome and courageous man who suddenly proclaimed himself King of the Jews. Simon sacked the royal palace of Jericho and burned a number of other palaces throughout the land until he was captured by the Roman procurator Gratus, who cut off his head.

There had also been a shepherd named Athronges. His main gifts seemed to be his great height, his immense physical strength, and his four stalwart brothers. Although these qualities fascinated

---

*Josephus, *History of the Jews.*

the adolescent Judas, he saw that however successful this keeper of sheep and goats was in gathering loyal partisans to foment righteous hatred against the soldiers of Herod and the Romans, it did not mean he deserved the title of King of the Jews, or Messiah.

Only moral perfection and purity of intention could justify violence. For the moment, it was Judas the Galilean who came closest to Judas's ideal. Yet the the Galilean was not a learned man. For Judas, the highest zeal for God and justice must be founded on a thorough and profound knowledge of the Torah and the other holy scriptures.

In fact, none of these warriors devoted sufficient time to study of the scriptures. Their invocations of the Holy Name as they went into battle seemed too much like a mere ritual cry. Their flesh, bones, and blood were not truly suffused with the holiness that would make them into a true arm of the wrath of God.

It was with great emotion that one Friday evening, shortly before the onset of the Shabbat, Judas received, from the hands of Judas the Galilean himself, his own dagger, the sica. This made him a Sicarius, a formal member of the Zealot group known as the Sicarii. He was struck by the curious resemblance between his own nickname, Judas of Keriot (his native town), and the new name that now applied to him: Judas Iscariot, or Judas the Sicarius. The "man from Keriot" was now the "man of the dagger."

He promised himself, however, that he would not use this weapon in the way so frequently resorted to by the Sicarii: One of them would infiltrate a noisy and bustling crowd in which an enemy of God, a Roman collaborator, or a teacher of heresy had been detected, sneak up behind the man, and stab him mortally. Then the Sicarius would cry "Murderer!" and slash the throat of another whom he had chosen as a scapegoat, creating a tumult and confusion from which he could flee at the first opportunity.

Judas did not approve of this practice. Stabbing someone in the back and murdering a scapegoat seemed unworthy of a pious man. He would have selected a nobler tactic: to approach the enemy, look him squarely in the eyes, and, instead of greeting him with a conventional embrace, stab him in the heart. Surely this was the only honest and religious way to do away with an enemy of the Chosen People.

As Judas the Galilean gave him his dagger, the Galilean did not speak at length, but pronounced these solemn words: "Know that from this moment on it is the hand of the Most High, the Almighty Judge, who holds this dagger. May your hand be his hand, and you shall see justice reborn in Israel and the reign of the Messiah."

At this moment, a story from scripture came to Judas's mind: It was Judas, son of Jacob, who had sold his brother Joseph for a few pieces of silver. Yet ultimately this could not be regarded as a crime, for it was this act that led to Joseph going into Egypt, which made him a savior of his people many years later.

Yes, YHWH does allow evil in the service of a greater good. "Thus he allows me to bear this dagger so that the poor and oppressed of Israel may reclaim their dignity someday," he thought. Inwardly, he felt he was authorized to shed blood for the Good Cause.

But Judas was intelligent and cautious. Was it not written never to invoke the name of God in vain? This holy name was for praise and worship alone, and woe unto him who used it only to justify his crime!

As he was mulling over these thoughts, an older man approached him. He was handsome and well built, with a calm face that contrasted with the tense and drawn features of those around him.

"My name is Simon, and I would like to speak with you. If you ever come to Capernaum, near the lake known as the Sea of Galilee, please come visit me. My house is not far from that of another Simon—a fisherman who is well known around there because everyone in the port has heard his thundering voice, especially when he quarrels with his wife, his daughter, or his mother-in-law. . . . But just ask for Simon the Zealot. That's what they call me there. You see, you and I are of the same family now, and I hope to see you soon!"

Judas smiled and gave fervent thanks to God. On this day, just before the holy Shabbat, he was not just receiving a dagger, a knife of justice. He felt he had also found a new father, one very different from his own blood father, yet one who also bore the name Simon.

"Simon the Zealot, you are my liberator on this day! Truly, the bonds of the heart and of sacred duty are deeper than the bonds of flesh. What is the fate imposed by nature beside the blessing that awaits us if we have the courage to liberate ourselves! I look forward to seeing you again soon, my father, my brother, my friend!"

And they embraced, as if to seal this mutual recognition and promise.

# 3

## *Capernaum*

After staying for several weeks with Judas the Galilean and his followers, Judas decided to leave them to visit Simon. He had been deeply touched by something in the man's look. Like Judas, he bore the dagger that made him a true Zealot. Yet Judas perceived no hatred in him and felt that this was a man who was capable of destroying the enemy without indulging in useless, negative emotions—neither hatred nor bloodthirsty pleasure, but simply for the sake of justice.

He had come to see the motivations of the Zealots he had met as far too influenced by politics. Was it really the Kingdom of God they were seeking or simply a better material world, without taxes—a peaceful life of work and family, interspersed with occasional visits to the Temple to salve their conscience, a type of comfortable conscience that is the very opposite of true religious conscience? It was true that they often spoke of the Messiah—but these were not men who ever woke up in the middle of the night, as Judas often did, because a voice was crying in their soul: "My Lord, and my God!"

It was with pleasure that Judas walked into Galilee. The country was beautiful and full of flowers, with many fertile orchards. He loved the colors and the taste of its fruits, a welcome change from the arid land of Judaea.

As he was going toward Jericho, he met two other travelers from Jordan who informed him that Yohanan the Baptist* had been arrested by Herod Antipas, the successor of Herod the Great, and that he was wasting away in prison.

Judas had heard of this Yohanan, whom the Zealots regarded as a prophet. He seemed to have the same conviction and moral force as those of their party, but his doctrine was weak and inconsequential, according to Judas the Galilean. Yohanan violently denounced the hypocrites, whether priests or Pharisees, rich or poor. But this was not enough. How could immersing people in water and converting them ever lead to driving the Roman occupiers out of Israel and restoring justice? What good was a virtue that had no arms to command respect?

Also, was not the fact of his arrest proof of his weakness? The only resistance he had to offer his persecutors were his pious prayers and his imprecations. Through his family, Judas knew much of the character of Herodias, Herod's wife, and had no doubt that Yohanan would be decapitated.

These two travelers tried to convince Judas that the sword of justice in the hands of an unjust man will only produce more injustice. They said that Yohanan was right when he preached that the true Holy War, the great one, is the war against the passions that disorient the heart and turn us away from the true path. They claimed that the Zealots were involved in a mere "small holy war"—and a mistaken one. "Violence cannot deliver us from violence," they said.

"Yes and no," Judas finally replied. "There is no small or great war. The only important consideration is the holiness of our intention."

---

*[John the Baptist.]

Judas and the two men continued on their way together, for the two travelers were going toward Tiberiade, only a few miles from Capernaum. They were greatly looking forward to seeing the Sea of Galilee. All three of these men from desert country rejoiced in the small miracles of wells, trees, and flowers.

As they walked, Judas was thinking of Yohanan. The Baptist was not an Essene, yet he seemed to have something strict and fierce in his attitude toward women, children, and the weak or infirm.

"How is he different from the Essenes?" Judas asked of his companions.

"Yohanan believes that human beings are not determined by the fate of their birth," one of them answered. "They can change and they can perfect themselves. They can be converted, which is symbolized by the sacred act of total immersion in water. The old life, with all of its bad habits, is washed away. It is purified and a new life begins. But the Essenes do not believe in this. For them, each of us is either born a 'son of Light' or a 'son of Darkness.' Nothing can change this. For them, there are only the elected and the rejected ones, the good and the bad, the pure and the impure."

"And who are the pure?" Judas asked.

"The Essenes, of course!" they answered. "Yohanan says that we are not predestined. Whatever the circumstances of our birth and the memories we carry within us, only a true and righteous life can make us pure."

"Pure and useless!" Judas answered bitterly. "Indeed, nothing good can come out of Judaea! Wandering ascetics who retire from the world, pure souls who do nothing about the poor dying of hunger and who surrender to the oppressor—these sons of Light are no better than sons of Darkness," he said, spitting on the ground.

It had long become clear from Judas's conversation that he was a Zealot. Yet his dissatisfation was also evident to the travelers.

"So, then, Judas—in your eyes, who has true grace? Your own

Zealot party seems to come up short as well. You are a true son of Israel who will not tolerate hypocrisy, half measures, or half truths. People like you must find themselves a little alone these days."

Judas immediately thought of Simon. "Perhaps not so alone," he said, with the hint of a smile on his lips, like a faint ray of hope.

The two men looked at each other and then revealed to Judas a strange event that had happened not long before Yohanan's arrest. When his cousin Yeshua* came to be baptized in the Jordan, Yohanan seemed deeply perturbed. Finally, he cried out: "It is not for me to purify you. I am unworthy to tie your sandals!" The travelers had not been able to hear what was said after this, but the atmosphere became very strange, with flocks of birds wheeling overhead. Some of Yohanan's disciples left him to follow this man Yeshua. Some of them were already saying that he was the long-awaited one.

Judas trembled. "Then he is the Messiah?"

The others dared not answer.

"Who can say? We do not know this man. Perhaps Yohanan had simply chosen him as his successor, because he's his cousin . . ."

"But Yohanan has never claimed to be the Messiah!"

"True enough, but he did say that he was sent to prepare the way for his coming."

"I think your desert ascetic is hallucinating from all his fasting. If the Messiah had really come, it would be obvious and known throughout the land! Even the infidels could not doubt it!"

"If we were incapable of doubt, we would no longer be human," one of the men replied.

This gave Judas pause for reflection. "It is true that since the beginning of creation, God himself has never tried to convince us of his existence. He leaves just enough traces in the sand for us to believe, and then sends just enough wind to erase them. Perhaps we are truly free, or perhaps life only gives us this illusion."

---

*[Throughout this text, Jesus will be called by his Aramaic name, Yeshua.]

Then the three said their farewells, for they had arrived at Tiberiade.

Judas spat on the ground as he passed the town, a city of vice built by Tiberius to rival the great imperial centers of iniquity! "May your dust soon return to dust!" he muttered.

Now alone, he quickened his pace toward Capernaum. Reaching the shore of the lake, he noticed a splendid villa near the town of Magdala. This must be the property of Lazarus of Bethany, a friend of his when they were studying together in Jerusalem. Lazarus had told him he often went to Magdala, accompanied by his parents and his two sisters, Martha and Miriam.

As he arrived in Capernaum, he heard a loud, braying voice, just as Simon had described it. Then he saw its source, a large, powerful man with prematurely white hair who was haranguing a crowd. Judas walked close to the man.

"He healed her! He healed her!" the man was shouting.

"Who?" Judas asked.

"My mother-in-law! She was burning with fever, and now she's skipping around like a girl!"

"Are you Simon?" Judas asked.

"How do you know me, stranger? Yes, I am Simon—to be more exact, Simon Peter, in service to the rabbi."

"What rabbi?"

"You don't know? Rabbi Yeshua of Nazareth, who interprets the Torah like a fresh fish so that its meat falls away from its bones by itself."

"Meat and bones of the Torah?"

"Yes, or, if you prefer, its Grace and its Law, or its Love and its Justice. It is only the edible parts we keep, you see," he said as if he were describing a meal.

Judas snorted. "If you separate the bones from the flesh, it is no longer a living fish, but a dead one."

"Ah, so you want the last word? You can have it. Keep it, along with your dead letters of scripture, full of bones. As for me, I am hungry for the living word!"

"How dare these ignorant fishermen interpret the Torah," Judas thought. Aloud, he said: "Before you get back to your fishing nets, Simon, tell me how to find the other Simon, the Zealot."

"A little farther that way, the fourth house on the right," Simon replied, with a large gesture and a friendly smile.

Judas was surprised at this. His words of contempt had met no contempt in reply. He was used to his unkind words being met by harder words in return, often with an insulting reference to his ugliness. Did not everyone see his ugliness as a punishment from God?

Simon the Zealot welcomed him with joy, but Judas found himself reserved, even mistrustful. How could he be joyous in a world so full of suffering and injustice?

"What kind of town is this?" Judas asked Simon. "I just made fun of an ignorant fisherman and he answered me with a great smile. And you seem so joyful, but how can you be? Surely this is not a time for joy. The time we live in is one for tears and anger. Shouldn't we reserve our joy for the time when the Messiah has come?"

"You don't know how right you are!" Simon the Zealot replied, laughing.

# 4

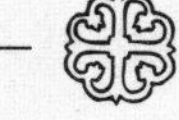

# *Teachings*

Judas was taken aback by the implications of Simon's words and attitude. This needed further questioning.

"What do you mean? Are you speaking of this rabbi of Nazareth? Do you really take him for the Messiah, the Messenger of God? Is he one of us?"

"There is no doubt about it," Simon replied. "Only yesterday I heard him say this to the crowd: 'Do not believe that I have come to bring peace on Earth. I bring not peace, but the sword. I have come to set son against father, daughter against mother, and daughter-in-law against mother-in-law. A person's own family shall be his enemies.'"

These words struck a deep chord in Judas, and reassured him. "Does he carry the dagger?"

"No. But his words cut deeper than the sharpest dagger! He has confronted the most eminent authorities, calling them 'whitewashed tombs' and 'ravaging wolves.' He has learned well the teaching of his cousin Yohanan, yet he is much clearer. 'Whoever is not with me is against me,' he says. And he also says, 'Whoever loves his father or his mother more than me is not worthy to be my disciple.'"

"So he really claims to be the Messiah!"

"Well, at any rate, he has the authority of the Messiah. No one has ever spoken like this man."

"But he seems to have no respect for the family. For most of us Jews, family is sacred."

"He speaks of another family. The other day, his brothers, his sisters, and his mother came to Nazareth, where he was preaching, and asked to speak to him privately. When he was informed of this, he exclaimed: 'Who are my mother, my sisters, and my brothers? My brothers and sisters are right here before me: those who live the Word of God. They are my true family.'"

Now Judas was thrilled. Finally, here was a teacher who did not exalt the family or domestic bliss or even happiness as the supreme goal of human life! Only one consideration troubled him about this man: Was he married? According to Jewish law, he would have to be if he was a real rabbi who teaches in the synagogue. An unmarried man is considered incomplete and is not allowed to teach there.*

When Judas alluded to this, Simon gave a coarse laugh. "Incomplete? I don't see how he could be, surrounded by all those beautiful women the way he is! But because we're on the subject, I must admit this is one of the few considerations about him that make me uncomfortable. It's not fitting for a warrior to be surrounded by women like that. It can only sap his vital force, given that women are not allowed to study scripture. But he says that women are like us, that God created us equal, to be side by side. Women are also waiting for the Messiah.

"But I haven't really answered your question because I'm not sure. He may or may not have a special woman companion, but it's

*See Jean-Yves Leloup, *The Sacred Embrace of Jesus and Mary* (Rochester, Vt.: Inner Traditions, 2006).

clear that he has preferences: That beauty called Miriam of Magdala seems especially intimate with him. She's also very intelligent—but she doesn't seem to use this intimacy to stand out from the other women. And Yeshua himself has said that he does not love Miriam more than Martha, Joanna, or Susanna. He clearly prefers her company, but he loves them all equally."

Judas was shocked by this kind of freedom. "But how does he deal with legitimate jealousy? Isn't he taking liberties with the Law? Isn't this just another case of choosing the scriptures we like and throwing out the rest?"

"Absolutely not," Simon replied. And he recounted what Yeshua said:

> Think not that I have come to abolish the law and the prophets; I have come not to abolish them but to fulfill them.
>
> For truly, I say to you, till heaven and earth pass away, not an iota, not a dot, will pass from the law until all is accomplished.
>
> Whoever then violates even the least of these commandments and teaches men to do so shall be called least in the kingdom of heaven; but he who practices them and teaches them shall be called great in the kingdom of heaven.*

Judas was reassured by these words. After a pause, Simon added:

"Fundamentally, Yeshua follows the Law, but in a different way. There seems to be more lightness in his way. For example, in his view, living with a woman is not an obligation or a duty, but a choice we make—out of happiness, perhaps . . ."

"Happiness?" Judas exclaimed. "What happiness can we expect from a woman? Pleasure, yes—but for how long? We are not mere animals! The burden of the Law must be heavy for us. How can he claim to make it light?"

---

*Matthew 5:17–19.

"By infusing it with love and consciousness," Simon answered gently.

"Love? What do you mean by that?" For Judas, this word had little meaning or significance.

"Is not our very first commandment that of love? 'You shall love the Lord your God with all your heart, your soul, and your might . . .'"

"Yes," Judas replied, "but isn't this commandment speaking of a difficult love, one that is a duty? I don't see anything light about it. If we do not love God, we shall be punished."

"Rabbi Yeshua says that love of God is not a duty, but an expression of our freedom, of our refusal to lose ourselves in the illusory realities of this ephemeral world. He says that the words 'You shall love' mean a process of becoming—not an obligation to be obeyed, but a hope."

"Hah! Now I begin to understand. Your Messiah is an artful musician! He has kept the words of the Torah but changed the melody. Simon, I confess I am at a loss. Your teacher both fascinates and repulses me. Tell me how I can meet him. I want to hear his music for myself and see whether it sounds false to my ears. I think already that it will, for great rigor and great lightness cannot go together. It seems to me that your Messiah has yet to make his choice between following happiness or following the Law. If so, he is only adding more trouble to our troubles. How many Roman soldiers has he rid us of and sent to the Valley of Gehenna? In spite of his righteous anger, this enchanting preacher of yours seems a little soft to me. How can I be sure he's not just another name to be added to the list of all those wretched pretender Messiahs?"

"Come and see for yourself," Simon replied.

# 5

# *Healing*

Simon thought to find Yeshua on the hill not far from the lake, where he liked to sit in the shade of the olive trees and teach his disciples. Yeshua preferred the open air and the company of trees, grass, and birds to the synagogues and halls of study.

People felt free to come to him with an empty purse or an empty head, for he spoke to the empty places in them. Whether the emptiness was felt in the stomach, the heart, or the head, his way was not to fill these spaces, but to make them even larger with his warm and luminous words. To be empty, full of space, nothing, was not a misfortune—such was to be a true human being, a nothingness made for God: "If I am nothing, all is there. God is All because he has nothing."

Of course this type of thinking was unfamiliar to Judas, and for that matter to the others gathered there. They were all too "full"—full of questions, emotions, pain, anger, darkness.

Then a man who had been blind from birth began to walk very slowly toward Yeshua. As Judas looked at the blind man, he wondered: Why do some people have to shut their eyes to keep from being blinded by the sun, while others have eyes that are always open, though no sun ever comes to disperse the perpetual night in which they are condemned to live? Some injustices were obviously man-made—all the Herods who had been murdering innocents for centuries—but there were also natural injustices: blindness, sickness, idiocy, and ugliness.

Judas sighed, feeling a familiar wave of despair. He felt he had the strength to combat man-made injustice, but how could he ever fight the injustices of nature? How can anyone fight a storm, a plague, or an earthquake that swallows the good along with the bad in one great convulsion? Again, the example of Job came to mind, he who had long felt like a brother to him. Was his destiny to be that of a Judas the Just, struggling against the injustice of God?

The blind man had now come close to Yeshua, and one of the disciples stopped him, taking his hand. In a loud voice, the disciple asked: "Rabbi, who is to blame that this man was born blind? Is the sin from him or from his parents?"*

The moment was so intense that Judas scarcely breathed. This was the central question that had haunted him his entire life. It was also the first time he had ever laid eyes on Yeshua, the one some called Teacher and others, such as Simon the Zealot, believed could be the Messiah.

Yeshua remained silent for a moment. Then he replied: "Neither from him nor from his parents."†

Seeing Judas's incredulity, Simon smiled. "That's his way—he often replies around the question and sometimes answers a question with another question. He prefers to deepen the mystery rather than explain it, you see. He will never give you an explanation or a solution, because then you'd have no more need to wonder. He always

---

*John 9:1–2.

†John 9:3. [This verse says: " . . . neither this man sinned [*hamartano*], nor his parents, but so that the works of God should be made manifest in him." —*Trans.*]

obliges you to think, because to think is to discover that the solution or the explanation that you thought you had is not the good one. For Yeshua, God is never the answer to our questions—he is the question to our answers."

"Neither his fault, nor that of his parents!" Judas interrupted, snorting in derision. "Then tell me, Simon, is there no cause at all for evil and suffering?"

"There is perhaps a cause, but no guilty being."

"No guilty being! What are you talking about? There has to be *some* guilty being—otherwise what is our armed struggle all about?"

"You see, Judas, already you are beginning to think!"

"I didn't need to come here for that! For many years, I have been asking this same question, and I always arrive at the same conclusion: It is useless to seek the ultimate cause of evil, for it always escapes us. Behind every cause you find, another is waiting, and no one dares to take it all the way back to the original cause, for fear of accusing God."

"Judas, this is blasphemy! Is God the cause of evil? Did the Creator himself make it so that this man would be born blind? Are you saying that he is the ultimate source of all of the world's suffering? Then how would you fight against God himself?"

"If I were a philosopher or pretending to be one, I'd have to reply that a human being can fight only against the secondary causes of evil, but the ultimate cause can be only God. If there is a guilty party, it is none other than he."

Simon began to tremble at the enormity of such blasphemy. At this moment, Yeshua arose and looked intently at the two men. Addressing Judas, he repeated: "Neither he nor his parents. Do not waste your time looking for the cause, for you will never find it. But especially do not waste your time looking for someone to blame. Instead, turn your attention to the victim. Take care of him, help him, and heal him." Then he paused, and added: "This sickness, this infirmity exists so that the glory of God may be manifest!"

Judas was so taken aback by this that he almost stumbled. These words seemed to reach him in a place the existence of which he had never been aware. Did evil and pain then have a meaning, a reason for being manifest?

Judas reflected. Yeshua was not simply invoking a final cause to replace the original cause. He spoke of "manifesting the glory," the fullness of the presence of YHWH, the One Who Is What He Is.

Were evil and misfortune therefore not mere quirks of fate, but a kind of opportunity or occasion? Was Yeshua saying that evil was an occasion for the manifestation of consciousness of dignity and of the grandeur of God—an occasion for a man to reveal himself as greater than his misery, his finitude . . . his ugliness, greater than "nature"?

Judas turned to Simon: "Was I born ugly so that I can manifest to everyone that I am not really ugly because I am *conscious* of my ugliness?"

"Judas, you're raving now. You're simply obsessed with your own problem."

"Am I? And what about my own mortality? Does my consciousness of my mortality manifest my immortality to everyone, because this consciousness cannot die? But what if this consciousness is itself mortal? Remember Ahitophel,* who first put his house in order, then hanged himself and died? Do you believe that his suicide manifested the power of his consciousness, which you call the glory of God?"

"Yes, I do," Simon answered. "There was still the presence of the consciousness and the breath inside the clay, the *adamah* of which we are made."

Judas was trembling because the story of the suicide of Ahitophel

*[In the Hebrew scriptures, Ahitophel (also Ahithophel) was a counselor of King David who turned against him and urged his rebel son, Absalom, to attack his father. But the counsel failed, and when Absalom was killed, Ahitophel first put his house in order and then hanged himself. —*Trans.*]

had always troubled him. But Simon was certainly right about one thing: This Yeshua did not answer people's questions; he gave them food for thought—but the thoughts seemed crazy or ridiculous to Judas.

Simon now spoke in a low voice. "Neither he nor his parents are to blame. This infirmity exists so that the glory of God may be manifest. Yeshua is saying that we must stop blaming others, the world, our parents, or even ourselves. In this way, misfortune becomes an opportunity for consciousness—and perhaps an opportunity for love. He also says: 'May those who have ears hear' and 'May those who have a heart understand.'"

But Judas could not or would not hear the word *love* in this. Perhaps this was what hid his deepest suffering: the impossibility that he could create in himself the love that he had always lacked.

The two friends were so involved in their conversation and reflections that at first they did not notice Yeshua lean over and mingle his saliva with a bit of dust and then apply two small poultices of the mud over the eyes of the blind man. But Judas was watching when Yeshua said: "Now, go and wash yourself, wash your eyes in the pond of Siloam."*

Judas himself volunteered to lead the blind man to the pool. Hand in hand, they walked in silence.

When the blind man finished washing his eyes, he could see. At this instant, Judas found himself struck by momentary blindness. Was it too much light or too much emotion?

Then he began to weep. He wept from joy, a joy he had never known before. Could this new joy possibly prevail in him? For a few seconds, Judas savored his blindness, and then he closed his eyes in utter happiness. He saw that the world was truly beautiful, that

*John 9:7.

everything was in its place and that his life leading up to this day had not been in vain. He forgot all his bitterness, his suffering . . . even the Herods, the Romans and their injustice, even all the injustices since the beginning of the world seemed to count for nothing now.

When a group who had been watching excitedly asked the blind man what had happened, Judas found himself murmuring the blind man's words of reply in unison with him: "The one called Yeshua made some mud and put it over my eyes, and told me: 'Go wash yourself.' I went and washed myself, and now my eyes can see."

Judas continued: "My eyes have seen you, Yeshua, my heart has recognized you. You are the most beautiful of the sons of man, and I am the ugliest of the sons of man. Together, we form the whole of humanity, the revelation of a greater God.

"Accept me as your disciple,
accept me, rather, as your other half,
for I am your shadow, and you are my Light.
I am the goat, you are the Lamb.
You are the Love that I lack, ignore, or suppress.
I have always known you,
and I am the flesh in which you incarnate,
I am the missing, really human part of you, Yeshua!
You are a complete man, but you lack only one thing: sin.
But it is sin that makes a man human.
It is his finitude, his erring, his desire.
It is that arrow that always aims aside,
missing its target as long as it has not found it.
Without this fault, this weakness,
why would we need salvation?
You say that you have not come for those who are well,
but for those who are sick.
You say you have come not for the just, but for the sinners.

You have come for me,
and without me you would not exist
or you would exist for nothing.
What would you and I be without each other?"

Judas was raving, no longer realizing what he was saying, and he stopped abruptly.

Yeshua stood before him, looking at him in total silence. In Yeshua's eyes, a kind of vertigo was manifest, as if he had just discerned a bottomless chasm in Judas. And in Judas's eyes, there was a matching vertigo, as if he had seen a bottomless chasm in Yeshua's eyes.

Whoever has contemplated this meeting of night and day would surely be able find other words to describe it beyond the dawn and the space containing them. But this meeting has remained without witnesses to tell of it.

As for Simon, he saw only Yeshua and Judas as two friends who are astonished to meet again after such a long absence.

# 6

## *One of the Twelve*

From now on, Judas walked with Yeshua. He was often silent, as if their dialogue continued in the shadows of the abyss where they had met and recognized each other. One day, Simon pointed out to Philip that these two men, outwardly so different, had a strange similarity. Each of them seemed to be constantly listening to some voice or inner presence, as if his behavior was guided by it, rather than by outer events or encounters. The source of each man's actions seemed to have an origin in something deeper than the human. Yeshua said he followed the will of his Father, but Judas did not speak of his Father. Was he following the Father, as Yeshua did, or another? It was as if Judas followed the dictates of some angel or demon that told him what he must do or say. Were they both following some destiny? It was as if the source of each man's action or inspiration left little to the free will either possessed, except the freedom to surrender to it. Yet is this not our only true freedom? To obey our destiny, to say yes to our true nature, to the moving tides that bear us? In any case, what use is it to struggle against the waves of this tide, except to smash the hull of our fragile ship?

The other disciples may often have felt at liberty to act as they pleased, but never Judas or Yeshua. It was as if each man had made a vow at birth to obey one voice that drowned out all other voices. It seemed clear to Simon that the voice Judas obeyed was that of justice. Yet Yeshua was a mystery to him, as he was to the others. There was something in him that escaped them—notions such as compassion, forgiveness, and mercy came to mind, but they could not yet find words to define it.

The disciples were surprised at the rapidity with which Judas seemed to win Yeshua's heart. Was it because he was so well educated, because he knew the Torah so well and was so adamant about living its precepts, or was it because he was a Judaean of aristocratic family, whereas many of them were only poor Galilean fishermen? "For us, the lake is our synagogue, and it is when we have a boat full of fish that we understand the beauty of which the scriptures speak," they joked.

As yet, no jealousy existed among them. All the disciples were dazzled and filled with gratitude just to be able to listen to the teaching of Yeshua.

Yet Yeshua himself was not unaware of some more attentive and comprehending ears among his disciples, of those who were prepared not only to espouse his teachings, but also to live them, and were ready to follow him all the way.

The time had come to initiate some of them into the secret of the Kingdom. With these select few, he would share his own intimacy with the one he referred to as his Father. As was his custom before making any important decision, he retired alone during an entire night to pray. He chose an isolated place not far from the lake, where there was a grotto he liked to visit when he wanted to be alone.

None could imagine the nature of his prayer there or his peculiar relationship with the one he sometimes called Abba, a name so intimate and familiar as to be startling when applied to YHWH, the Creator of all that lives and breathes.

"Abba"—occasionally some of the disciples had heard him whisper this word. Could Yeshua be thinking about his father, Joseph, and missing him, or was he simply a bit crazy? But perhaps this whisper signified one of those moments, so frequent with him, when all creation became familiar, when the heavens seemed to have descended upon earth, when time and eternity were no longer separate, when the abyss that separated the divine from the human disappeared.

When he returned to Capernaum, Yeshua gathered together his men and women disciples, along with his mother and his brothers and sisters, who had come from Nazareth. Among the men, Yeshua chose twelve. This figure appealed to him because it symbolized the twelve tribes of Israel, the twelve months of the year, and the twelve signs of the zodiac. But he said nothing of this to them. People in those times generally knew that the figure four symbolized the world of space, associated with the earth, and the figure three symbolized sacred time, associated with the heavens. The multiplication of these two figures thus symbolized the origin of the world. Hence, this figure also indicated Yeshua's intention: to fulfill the created world by establishing a communion and fusion between it and the uncreated, to make a "new earth and a new heaven." It was this that he meant by the Kingdom: the reign of spirit in the human heart, which could give rise to a totally different world.

He called them each in turn by their names: Simon the fisherman (who would become Peter); Andrew, his brother; James and John (Yohanan), the sons of Zebedee; Philip; Bartholomew; Thomas; Matthew; James, the son of Alphaeus; Thaddeus; Simon the Zealot; and Judas Iscariot. To these men he formally transmitted the power to banish unclean spirits so as to heal all sickness and despondency.

The disciples rejoiced in receiving this power. Each had his own ideas as to the nature of demons and what was necessary to exorcise them, to drive them from the manifest world so that it regained its true nature, a realm of beauty and peace.

Among his women disciples, Yeshua chose Susanna, Salome, Joanna, and Miriam of Magdala. Most of them, like the wife of Herod's steward, were women of wealth and standing. They helped the disciples materially, but even more with their patience and kindness.

These men and women knew that they were part of an inner circle, but they also realized what grave responsibilities this carried and a commitment that might be beyond their strength. They trembled before the enormity of mission that Yeshua, the Teacher, had conferred upon them:

> Go not to the Pagans, and enter no town of the Samaritans,
> But go rather to the lost sheep of the house of Israel.
> And preach as you go, saying, "The kingdom of heaven is at hand."
> Heal the sick, raise the dead, cleanse lepers, cast out demons. You received without paying, give without pay.
> Take no gold, nor silver, nor copper in your belts, no bag for your journey, nor two tunics, nor sandals, nor a staff; for the laborer deserves his food.
> And whatever town or village you enter, find out who is worthy in it, and stay with him until you depart.
> As you enter a house, bless it.
> And if the house is worthy, let your peace come upon it; but if it is not worthy, let your peace return to you.
> And if any one will not receive you or listen to your words, shake off the dust from your feet as you leave that house or town.
> Truly, I say to you, on the day of judgment it shall be easier for the land of Sodom and Gomorrah than for that town.

Behold, I send you out as sheep in the midst of wolves; so be wise as serpents and innocent as doves.

Beware of men; for they will deliver you up to councils, and flog you in their synagogues, and you will be dragged before governors and kings for my sake, to bear testimony before them and the Gentiles.

When they deliver you up, do not be anxious how you are to speak or what you are to say; for what you are to say will be given to you in that hour;

For it is not you who speak, but the Spirit of your Father speaking through you.

Brother will deliver up brother to death, and the father his child, and children will rise against parents and have them put to death; and you will be hated by all for my name's sake. But he who endures to the end will be saved.

When they persecute you in one town, flee to the next; for truly, I say to you, you will not have gone through all the towns of Israel, before the Son of Man comes.

A disciple is not above his teacher, nor a servant above his master;

It is enough for the disciple to be like his teacher, and the servant like his master. If they have called the master of the house Beelzebub, how much more will they malign those of his household.

So have no fear of them; for nothing is veiled that will not be revealed, or hidden that will not be known.

What I say to you in the darkness, speak it in the light; and what you hear whispered, proclaim it from the rooftops.

And do not fear those who kill the body but cannot kill the soul; rather fear him who can destroy both soul and body in hell.

Are not two sparrows sold for a penny? Yet not a single sparrow
falls to the ground without your Father's knowledge.
And you: Even the hairs of your head are all numbered.
Therefore be without fear; for you are of more value than many
sparrows.
So every one who acknowledges me before men, I also will
acknowledge before my Father who is in heaven; but whoever denies me before men, I also will deny before my Father
who is in heaven.
Do not think that I have come to bring peace on earth; I have
not come to bring peace, but a sword.
For I have come to set son against his father, and daughter
against mother, and daughter-in-law against her mother-in-law;
And a man's foes will be those of his own household.*

The chosen disciples were overwhelmed by the implications of such a mission. But the breath of Yeshua filled and inspired them. They knew it was not by their own strength that they could accomplish all this, but rather with his strength and that of the Father in them all. Privately, they all prayed that their faith and confidence in him and his presence in their innermost being would never leave them.

On that day, Miriam had prepared a delicious meal, and as they ate, all the inner circle rejoiced in being chosen by him whom some already regarded as not only their Teacher and Master, but also the Messiah foretold by the prophets.

At the end of the meal, however, Yeshua spoke some strange words, directed primarily to the men. It was as if he were confiding in them as he said: "It is not you who have chosen me, but I who have chosen you. And among you, I have chosen a demon."

---

*Matthew 10:5–33.

What on earth could he mean? How was it possible that Yeshua had chosen a demon as one of his closest disciples? What could this demon's mission possibly be? Perhaps a demon's help was sometimes necessary to exorcise other demons? They puzzled greatly over this. They could not help but be reminded of accusations that had already been made against Yeshua himself: that he was possessed by Beelzebub, for only the prince of demons can expel demons.*

*Matthew 3:12.

# 7

## *A Demon*

As the days went by, the words of Yeshua still troubled and astonished the disciples. Had he not rebuked those who accused him of being a demon?

> How can Satan cast out Satan? If a kingdom is divided against itself, that kingdom cannot stand. And if a house is divided against itself, that house cannot stand.*

> And if I cast out demons by Beelzebub, by whom do your sons cast them out? Therefore they shall be your judges. But if it is by the Spirit of God that I cast out demons, then the kingdom of God has come unto you.†

But these words were far from comforting to them. They only raised more troubling questions: "Could I be the one? Could you be

*Mark 3:23–25.

†Matthew 12:27–28.

the one?" Some even felt that Yeshua's words had sown doubt and suspicion among them.

Seeing how troubled they were, John reprimanded them: "Does a gardener keep a rotten fruit in the same basket as good fruits? If he does, the whole basket will turn rotten. No! I cannot believe he means there is a Satan among us."

Judas answered him with a smile: "Who created Satan, then? Did God not intend him for a special purpose, for the greater good of all? Read the scriptures again, Yohanan. Do you not remember the Book of Job, in which Satan is a son of God whose function is to test the just man in order to reveal what is in the depths of his heart, his head, his gut? Satan's function is to test the truth and the character of each of us. Does his name not signify 'obstacle'? Without obstacles, without trials, how can we truly know ourselves and grow?"

And then he added: "Satan is God himself."

This was too much for Yohanan and Simon Peter. "Stop!" they cried in unison. "That is blasphemy!"

"It is clear that you are ignorant of the scriptures," Judas replied. "Just read the Book of Numbers:

> And an angel of God came upon the road
> *Vayitatzev Malak Hakhem borderer*
> as an obstacle to him
> *Le-satanne lo.**

"Does this passage not clearly say that an angel of God came upon the road as Satan?"

---

*Numbers 22:22. [Another frequent translation of the Hebrew word *satan* is "adversary." In André Chouraqui's translation of Numbers 22:32, the angel says, "I myself have come here as Satan." I am unable, however, to find any passage in the Book of Numbers corresponding to Judas's further claim that God himself says this. —*Trans.*]

"What—Satan an angel of God?" the two exclaimed. "You frighten us, Judas!"

Judas replied calmly, "If you read a little farther on, the scripture says:

> Lo, it is I who have come to prevent him;
> *Nine Anohi yatzati le Satanne;*
> Lo, it is I [*anohi*], for it is I (the Eternal One, your God)
> who have come to be Satan . . ."*

Judas continued: "In the first verse I quoted, Satan is an angel; in the second, God himself says he is Satan."

Now the two other disciples were silent.

Judas began to laugh. "Come, come, now don't be afraid! God and Satan are names that we give to the One Reality. This One Reality makes us laugh, makes us weep, makes us flourish, and makes us wither and die. If your God is only light and not darkness, it is a false God. Where do you think darkness comes from? If our God is only good, then why is there Evil? You must not make God according to your image of your own best qualities. Never forget the horrors of which you are capable! Is God not there also?"

Then he turned away and began to murmur to himself in a whisper so low they could not hear: "A Messiah who is only light and goodness would be an illusion, for he would incarnate an incomplete God, a God who is less than All. I, Judas, will help him to be complete. If sin is absent from him, then he lacks the element that makes a man truly human. I will be the evil that is lacking in him, so as to be God, the totality of All. . . . Yes, my luminous Yeshua, you cannot be God without your shadow, Judas. . . ."

---

*Numbers 22:32.

Miriam had been listening attentively to this exchange. Seeing that Yohanan and Simon Peter were deeply troubled, she approached them and said, "The God of which Judas speaks is not the One who guides Yeshua. Yes, his God includes the Divine, all the greatness of nature, with its shadows and light, its beautiful day and strange night, its catastrophes, its flowers, the laughter of children as well as the cries of the murdered. And if God were *only* this All, Judas would be right; for it is true that good and evil are not enemies— they are complementary.

"Yet when Yeshua says there is a demon among us, I do not believe this is what he means. If there is a demon, it is because Yeshua has chosen him to be among us. It is because of his own choice. The Divine All does not choose anything—it simply allows everything to exist. Nature does not choose; she makes everything flourish. She intoxicates us with the perfume of her roses and wounds us with their thorns, she produces the sweetest tastes and the most violent poisons. By making his choice, Yeshua is bearing witness that God is a being who chooses. This is what is so hard for us to understand and accept. We would prefer a Divine that is choiceless, an impersonal Divine upon which we can project the best of ourselves. But God is more than simply the Divine. God is the freedom within this Divine. God is Someone, and Yeshua is also Someone, and he has chosen us.

"As for us, we can refuse this choice, we can refuse to be loved among all men and all women. And this is where the demon is: in the possibility of refusing this gift of love, of saying no to love. It is this demon who renounces love, for he no longer believes in it."

But Simon Peter was shaking with anger. "Be quiet, woman! Who are you to presume to teach us? Are you not inhabited by the demon of pride?"

"You are right, my brother!" she answered. "But do not fear this demon of pride, for it is a demon that can be converted and forgiven. This demon can humble itself before a love greater than its vanity, its fear, or its violence.

"But the demon among us that Yeshua speaks of is not just 'one of us,' though it may have to be one of us who manifests it. If Yeshua had not chosen us, we would not have the possibility of refusing his choice. We are all demons, inasmuch as we are free individuals who have witnessed his love and refused to believe in it. And this is why people prefer the Divine to God: The Divine does not look us directly in the eye, the Divine has no face that questions us with great, open eyes. The Divine is the fate that befalls us, yet it has no hand to raise us up from it."

# 8

# *The Wild Ass*

Judas had also been listening attentively to the words of Miriam and was irritated by them. The love he felt for Yeshua was his fate and his destiny. Why speak of freedom with regard to it? Judas's own choice in the matter counted for nothing; he was powerless to resist this love. Above all, he was certain that he would never betray Yeshua. In this, he thought exactly as Simon Peter did: "All others may forsake him, but never me!" Only cowards had the freedom to betray. For him, the righteous ones (and not just among his party of the Zealots) held to the solemn vow "Better to die than to betray!" Judas was certain of himself in this matter. Now, he began to wonder if Miriam might not be the demon of whom Yeshua spoke. Was she not spreading doubt and mistrust by harping on this possibility of choice, of refusal of love?

Thus Judas and Simon Peter had two important character traits in common: Each was certain that he could never betray Yeshua; and each had a deep-seated mistrust of women, those "tools of Satan." Yet in all other respects they were very different. In fact, one consideration that struck everyone was the great diversity among those chosen by Yeshua. He was the Teacher who brought unity to the group, yet no member felt he was being asked to renounce his or her difference from the others.

Judas and Yohanan were the only men in the group without female companions. For Yohanan, the reason was mostly his youth, but it was also because his love for Yeshua seemed enough to fill his heart. As for Judas, he had left his wife—a woman he had married only to become a rabbi and teach in the synagogues.

Judas had not been able to tolerate living with this woman. The last straw was when she told him one day that she detested him and the Law that required them to live together when they did not love each other. This was sufficient blasphemy in Judas's eyes to provide an excuse for sending her back into the streets, where he had found her. Customs were often crude then, and the Law of Moses could not prevent certain excesses.

Yeshua had fulfilled this requirement of the scriptures, and Judas respected him for it, but he found it difficult or impossible to imagine his Teacher's private life in this regard. Nor did the other disciples presume to imagine Yeshua's sexual life. A divinely incarnated human or the Messiah would surely not have Judas's own torment regarding sexual pleasure, but on the other hand, this Messiah would not be a man if he had not known a woman. He would be a man without God, because in some rabbinic teachings, sexuality was said to be the presence of the Divine in our flesh, the possibility of engendering a new life . . . but those particular teachings made Judas laugh. The presence of the Divine in our flesh? Then it must be the same for animals! And did animals that copulated and reproduced more frequently than humans have more of the Divine in them?

Judas, as it turned out, was more than passing familiar with animal sexuality. Yohanan had nicknamed him "the wild ass" ever since he and Peter had heard him "braying" from a distance. But was Judas engaged in the act of coupling with a woman, or with a she-goat?

No one dared ask the question or even think much about it. In any case, none of them could imagine Judas's misery with regard to sexuality. "Even the women I offer to pay refuse me," he said to himself bitterly. "And if they do accept, they simply present themselves to me from behind, like animals, so as not to have to lie face-to-face with me. For me, the act of sex has no human face, anyway—why should anyone begrudge me if I turn to animals?"

Only once had a woman said to him, "Look me in the eyes!" But this invitation stunned Judas so much that he was impotent. It seemed that the love between man and woman that is transmitted through the eyes was not for him, not for the wild asses. That kind of love was reserved for the likes of Yeshua and Miriam. These two had only to allow their looks to mingle for their very bodies to seem to fill to overflowing with a dewy tenderness. Judas would have liked very much to experience this kind of erotic gift, which is not mere discharge, but instead sexuality with a face and a heart. But ever since his adolescence, it had been denied him, yet another injustice that seared his soul with sadness and his body with outrage.

Strangely, the only woman who seemed to show understanding and respect for him was Miriam of Magdala. She had known men like Judas before. She was no stranger to the language of sighs and cries, and she knew only too well the role of woman in her society: to make men feel like gods so that they did not become (or remain) beasts. But Judas had never loved a woman and it was much too late for him now. He had learned to content himself with rapid acts of discharge, with whoever—or whatever—was available. Long ago, he had chosen to sublimate most of this energy into the pleasures of politics and battle. He had long ago decided to devote himself to preparing the way for the Messiah, but he wanted a Messiah who shared his own vehement commitment to one goal—the restoration of the Kingdom of God in Israel—and this required the fall of the Herods and the end of imperial Roman rule and law, for Israel could have no master other than Yahweh and no law but that of the Torah.

In his time among the Zealots, he had acquired a new taste for human company, with evenings around the fire, the strong odors of sweat and breath that smelled of garlic and fish, and the wine of Cana, which seemed to him more savory than any woman's perfume.

He had taken note of one thing the Teacher said: "There are those who are born from their mother's womb as eunuchs, there are those who are made eunuchs by other men, and there are those who make themselves eunuchs for the sake of the Kingdom of Heaven."* This inspired him to become the last: Instead of continuing to find release with prostitutes or animals, he vowed to master his own body.

He was surprised, however, that Yeshua himself did not follow this path of sexual abstinence, as did some of his Essene friends. Probably it was so that he might "fulfill the Law" without omitting one iota of it. Nevertheless, the Teacher had made it clear by his own words that he did not condemn this practice (familiar to certain pagan sects but strange to most Jews) of sacred celibacy. Hence, Judas could practice it without feeling he was doing something wrong.

Because of his decision, to see Yeshua so often surrounded by women disturbed Judas, and it began to cause him to feel something worse than discomfort: the beginnings of doubt and even of suspicion. How could a righteous rabbi offer his teaching to women, whom the Torah of Moses has judged unworthy and incapable of understanding it? If Yeshua had to have a woman companion to fulfill the Law, why did he not leave her at home? Her proper place was there, not in the synagogues or walking the roads of Galilee side by side with him! A rabbi who had women disciples was no longer a rabbi. Perhaps Yeshua believed, however, that one of the functions

---

*Matthew 19:12.

of the Messiah was to abolish all these exclusions and limits created by limited minds. In the same way that he made no distinction between rich and poor, perhaps he no longer saw males and females, but rather persons. But how far would he go in this? Would he also accept as disciples foreigners, pagans, and enemies of Israel?

One day, he approached Yeshua, and quoted this passage of scripture:

> My son, be attentive to my wisdom, and turn your ear to my understanding. May you follow the way of prudence . . . for the lips of a strange woman drip honey, and her tongue is smoother than oil; but in the end she is bitter as wormwood, sharp as a two-edged sword. Her feet walk the way down to death, her steps lead to hell. She is heedless of the path of life, for she goes astray, and does not know it.*

Yeshua answered him only with silence.

But the hardest thing for Judas to accept was the way Yeshua would often kiss Miriam on the mouth.† Every time Judas happened to observe them in this attitude of abandon and self-offering, he felt sick to his stomach.

---

*Proverbs 5:1–6.

†See Jean-Yves Leloup, *The Gospel of Philip* (Rochester, Vt.: Inner Traditions, 2004), page 83, plate 111.

# 9

# *The Gospel according to Judas*

But in spite of Yeshua's love of the company of women, his words were very much that of a virile man. There were times when his words seemed violent, even like those of a Zealot. These were the times when Judas was reassured and filled with admiration. Because he was the only highly educated man among the twelve disciples, he took upon himself the task of writing down these sayings of the Teacher. Someday, people would need a record of Yeshua's teaching. For Judas, this rabbi from Nazareth was indeed the long-awaited Righteous One, foretold by the prophets, and a strict interpreter of the Law, filled with righteous zeal for the restoration of Israel.

1. Saying of Yeshua
Do not believe that I have come to abolish the Law or the prophets. I have come not to abolish, but to fulfill them. I tell you, not a *yod* nor an *iota* shall be erased from the Law. He who neglects the least of the teachings and teaches others to do the same is no longer guided by the spirit.

2. Saying of Yeshua
They have said to you: "You shall not commit adultery." But I tell you, whoever looks at a woman with lust has already committed adultery with her.

3. Saying of Yeshua
If your right eye is the cause of sin, tear it out and throw it far away. If your right hand is the cause of sin, cut it off and throw it far away. For it is better that you lose part of your body than for your whole body to go to Gehenna.

4. Saying of Yeshua
You cannot serve two masters. If you are attached to one, you will scorn the other. You cannot serve both God and Mammon.

5. Saying of Yeshua
Whoever listens to what I say and does not practice it is like a madman who builds his house on sand.

6. Saying of Yeshua
Foxes have their dens and the birds of the sky have their nests, but the Son of Man has no place to rest his head.

7. Saying of Yeshua
Do not believe I have come to bring peace on earth, for I bring the sword. I have come to set son against father, daughter against mother, and daughter-in-law against mother-in-law. Your enemies shall be the members of your own family.

8. Saying of Yeshua
If anyone comes to me who does not hate is father, his mother, his wife, his children, his brothers, his sisters, and even his own life, he

is not my disciple. Whoever cannot abandon all he has cannot be my disciple.

9. Saying of Yeshua
You are those who appear just in the eyes of men. But YHWH knows your hearts: What is highly esteemed by men is an object of disgust for YHWH.

10. Saying of Yeshua
It is the violent ones (the Zealots) who will possess the Kingdom of God.

11. Saying of Yeshua
You hear, but you do not understand.
You look, but you do not see.
Your mind is dull,
your ears are deaf, your eyes are closed
from fear of what your eyes may see,
from fear of what your ears may hear,
from fear of what your mind might understand
and thereby convert you.

12. Saying of Yeshua
This people honor me with their lips,
but their hearts are far from me.
The worship they offer me is vanity,
the doctrines they teach are only human precepts.

13. Saying of Yeshua
Whoever wants to save his life will lose it. Whoever loses his life for my sake will find it. What use is it for a man to win the whole world, if he ruins his own life?

14. Saying of Yeshua
I tell you, it will be difficult for a rich man to enter the Kingdom of Heaven! Yes, I repeat: It is easier for a camel to pass through the eye of a needle than for a rich man to enter the Kingdom of Heaven.

15. Saying of Yeshua
Woe unto you, hypocrite scribes and Pharisees, who close the Kingdom of Heaven to men. You cannot enter it yourselves and you obstruct those who want to enter it.

16. Saying of Yeshua
Woe unto you, hypocrite scribes and Pharisees, who resemble whitewashed tombs: Their outside appears beautiful, but their inside is full of rotting bones.

17. Saying of Yeshua
You generation of vipers! How will you escape the wrath that is coming?

18. Saying of Yeshua
Beware! For you know neither the day nor the hour. If the master of the house knew when the thief was coming, he would be prepared, and not allow the wall of his house to be breached.

19. Saying of Yeshua
Woe to you rich men; you have your consolation.
Woe to you whose bellies are always full; you will go hungry.
Woe to you who laugh now; you will know weeping and sorrow.
Woe to you when people praise you; this is indeed how their fathers greeted the false prophets.

20. Saying of Yeshua
The light came into the world, and people preferred the shadows to the light, for their hearts were wicked. Indeed, whoever commits evil hates the light and will not come into it for fear that his guilty deeds will be exposed.

21. Saying of Yeshua
If God were your Father, you would love me, for I am of God and have come from him. I did not come of myself, for it is he who sent me.

Why do you not recognize my way of speaking? It is because you cannot hear my words. You come from your father, the devil, and it is his wishes you want to fulfill. He was a murderer from the beginning and did not dwell in the truth, for there was no truth in him. When he offers you lies, he offers his own substance, for he is a liar and the father of lies.

Because I speak the truth, you do not believe me. Who among you will convict me of sin? If I speak the truth, why do you not believe me? Whoever is of God understands the word of God. If you do not understand me, you are not of God.

22. Saying of Yeshua
Beware lest they deceive you. For many will come in my name and will say; I am the Messiah, and they will deceive many people. You will also hear war and rumors of war, but do not be afraid, for all this must be accomplished, yet it is not the end. Nation shall rise against nation . . . there will come famines and earthquakes. But all of this will only be as the beginning of labor pains. False prophets will spring up in great numbers and will mislead many. Because of the growing wickedness, love will grow cold in most people, but those who hold firm until the end will be saved. This good news will be proclaimed throughout the world. And then will come the end.

Judas had noted many other sayings of Yeshua, but he preferred words such as these, words of curses rather than blessings. The love of the justice and judgment of YHWH was the only good news for him. He wrote down not Yeshua's words that offered compassion and forgiveness, but those that made great demands. Occasionally, words of great intransigence and even violence would come from the mouth of the Teacher, and it was these that Judas selected. He did not write down his words of kindness, patience, and hope.

# 10

## *Yeshua the Zealot*

Though he carefully noted these words of Yeshua, it was the Teacher's actions that he most admired—a striking contrast to the Pharisees, who "speak, but do not act." Yeshua practiced what he preached, he said what he thought, and his thought arose from his true being. Being, thought, words, and actions were one with him. The more Judas lived alongside Yeshua, the more fascinated he was by the Teacher. His passion for Yeshua verged on worship, though he was stopped sharply from this by recalling that only YHWH, the One Who Is What He Is, deserved worship. But there was one moment of exaltation so great for Judas that he could not help falling upon his knees before Yeshua: when the Teacher came to cleanse the Temple.

It was Passover, and they had come to Jerusalem. Yeshua and his disciples climbed up the hill to the Temple, which they found occupied by sellers of cattle, sheep, and doves to be used in sacrifice, and by money changers who sat comfortably, driving hard bargains to get a high price for their money. The noise of their haggling was so loud that it almost drowned out the voice of the Teacher as he reminded the money changers that this was a house of prayer and not of commerce. One of these retorted that his commerce was more effective than prayer because it enabled all this animal flesh to be transformed into burnt offerings to God.

Judas replied vehemently: "What sort of God takes pleasure at seeing the bloodshed of innocent animals? This blood enriches only the high priests and their families. They and all their rabble serve the villainous Caesar, not God!"

Yeshua saw that no words would reach the hearts of these men. Then, possessed by that quiet rage known only to the just, he seized a rope used to attach cattle and made a knotted whip of it, then he flung the whip about in great circles, scattering the tables and the coins of the merchants. Not stopping there, he also attacked the animal sellers, scattering their cattle, sheep, and doves in a great chaos. Judas thought of using his dagger, but for now was content to lend a hand to Yeshua, rushing about and shoving aside people and obstacles. Yet all the other disciples stood as if frozen in awe of all this force and violence coming from the two men. They remembered the words that were written: "Zeal for your house will consume me."*

Faced with this catastrophe, the merchants ran to appeal to the priests. One of them arrived and asked Yeshua: "Who are you, to act in this way?"

Judas was about to exclaim, "He is the prophet, the Messiah spoken of in the scriptures! Kneel before him!" but Yeshua sensed this and silenced him with a gesture. Then he answered the priests: "Destroy this sanctuary, and I will rebuild it in three days."†

The priests answered him: "It took forty-six years to build this sanctuary, and you claim you can rebuild it in three days?" But Yeshua meant the sanctuary of his own body, the body and heart of a human

---

*John 2:17.

†John 2:19.

being. He was saying that this is the true sanctuary that must be delivered from all the calculating and bargaining to be a true offering to YHWH. It must become a space of silence and, as is said in the Book of Wisdom, "a place for his repose."

He also announced that if his body was destroyed, it would not die, for after death it would "stand straight and high."* Death comes only to that which is mortal, not the everlasting I AM, which is eternal life. But they did not understand what he was talking about, and very few of his hearers were able to grasp the symbolic and initiatory dimension of his words.

Though Judas stood right next to his Teacher, he missed his meaning. Instead, he took his words literally: Yeshua was going to destroy this unclean Temple and build a new one in its place, which only the pure, those filled with zeal for the House of God, would be allowed to enter.

Because Yeshua was of David's lineage, he could sit on the throne of David. Like the messiah-king of those glorious days, he would restore the reign of Law and justice in Israel. Undoubtedly, he would appoint Judas as his minister in gratitude for his having been the only one with the courage to support him in his combat against the injustice in the Temple. With Judas as minister, he could be sure that the Law would be respected and that the Temple would truly be the Temple of God, a house of prayer reserved for pious Jews.

Judas never could have imagined that Yeshua's actions might have the opposite meaning: that he wanted to liberate the "pagan square" of tenants and merchants of only one religion. For Yeshua, the presence of YHWH was not something reserved for Jews only: "My house shall be known as a house of prayer for all peoples." By his actions, Yeshua was rather reminding the Jews that they were not

---

*This is the original meaning of the Greek word *anastasis*, generally translated as "resurrection."

a people chosen for themselves, for their own exclusive welfare, but to serve as a people who transmit and share the holy gift: an openness to transcendence. Their religion and their Law should serve as rays of light that illuminate the otherwise dense and opaque flesh of the world.

But Judas wanted to see Yeshua only as a man who was strong and certain in his mission, a man who could drive Caesar out of the land and take his place. His Teacher's words that Judas heard and understood and the acts he witnessed and approved confirmed his conviction: This was the Messiah, the pious and powerful Zealot for whom they had been longing.

# 11

## *The Adulteress*

Nevertheless, the strong, pure, and perfect man whom Judas so admired turned out to have certain weaknesses, especially regarding women. It was an encounter with an adulteress who had been caught in the act that was the occasion of their first quarrel.

Some scribes and doctors of the Law had brought the woman before Yeshua. They made her stand so that everyone could see her ridiculous attire, which was so revealing as to be obscene.

"Rabbi, this woman was caught in a flagrant act of adultery. In the Torah, Moshe himself has declared that the punishment for such action is stoning to death. What do you say?"

Judas could barely restrain himself from exclaiming, "What are you waiting for? It is written: You should stone her, as you should have already stoned the adulterer!"

But Yeshua was silent. He squatted and began drawing figures with his finger in the sand.

Judas thought that surely he could not ignore the scriptures that prescribe in great detail the proper behavior for a member of the Chosen People, especially in such matters. What made this people different had to be manifest in their everyday behavior, otherwise they would be just another nation among the nations. If they could not eat what they pleased or how they pleased, then surely they could not have sex with anyone they pleased, anytime they felt like it! Was it not written: "You shall not behave as people in the land of Egypt, where you have lived; nor shall you behave as those in the land of Canaan"?*

Adultery was an affront to Israel's holiness and a mortal insult to the spirit of its fathers. This was why the act was serious enough to merit the death penalty.

> If a man commits adultery with the wife of his neighbor, both the adulterer and the adulteress shall be put to death.
>
> If a man lies with a male as with a woman, both of them have committed an abomination; they shall be put to death, their blood is upon them.
>
> The man who lies with his father's wife has uncovered his father's nakedness; both of them shall be put to death, their blood is upon them.
>
> If a man or woman lies with a beast, they shall be put to death; and you shall kill the beast.†

Hence the sentence for this woman was clear: God himself had prescribed it through the mouth of Moses:

> If a man is found lying with the wife of another man, both of them

---

*Leviticus 18:3.

†Selections from Leviticus 8.

> shall die, the man who lay with the woman, and the woman. Thus you shall purge the evil from Israel.*

Familiar as he was with these texts, Judas was oblivious as to how at least one of them might apply to his own transgressions.

Yeshua's silence and hesitation were strange and disturbing to him. Why was he squatting on the ground with his head lowered like that? He would not even look the woman in the eyes, as the others did, already stoning her with their stares, in which a mixture of hatred and lust could be detected. Why did Yeshua not look evil in the face now? What was he doing, scribbling like that in the sand?

But Yeshua knew that YHWH does not merely look at facial expressions. God sees beyond the human masks of pleasure and pain, all the way to the true face, "made in his own image . . ."

Yeshua was certainly able to see the evil in this woman, but unlike the others, he did not merely see an adulteress; he saw a woman, a human being. Where the others saw a caricature, he saw a true face beyond the outer face. And in this moment, while all the others were restless and shouting, it was as if Yeshua and the woman were alone together and silent, suffering together.

Yeshua perceived how utterly miserable a creature this woman was. Yet he also acknowledged a kind of courage in her engaging in such an act, knowing full well the gravity of the risk she was taking. In some part of her, she was willing to risk death in her desperate desire to find love. Had she found love with the man with whom she had committed adultery? Had she been granted a taste, however fleeting, of that life which makes us forget death and its domain? Was not this woman a symbol for all of humanity, searching elsewhere for happiness and love because we cannot find it in ourselves? "He has come into the world not to judge it or condemn it, but so that the world may be saved." What was adultery if not

*Deuteronomy 22:22.

self-deception, searching for happiness away from God, searching for love in ways that bring only sorrow? For this love, this happiness that people lust after, has nothing of Being itself, of the Infinite. And no finite being, however great, can ever plumb the depths of this Infinity. As long as human beings fail to turn to God to find God, they can be only adulterers. They can be only unhappy creatures, because they mistake other creatures for the Creator.

There Yeshua sat, in the midst of these men, a Teacher who had come to show them what real happiness was, what real goodness was, and to save them from illusion.

But Judas had no interest in any salvation that would not drive out the Roman occupiers. Today, his Teacher seemed disconcertingly like some sort of philosopher. Had he forgotten that he was a prophet of God? People did not look to the Messiah for that soft and compliant silence of a philosopher! The Messiah was supposed to be the Messenger of that God of righteousness and wrath who would avenge and purify his people and his land of all forms of sin.

Judas could never have imagined how weary Yeshua had become of all the obsessive Jewish rules about eating, drinking, and sexual behavior. The essence of Judaism was surely elsewhere! To the pure, all is pure. And to those with a corrupt heart, all is impure. How many human embraces, even lawful ones, had been corrupted by lack of love? How many couples slept in the same bed without ever sharing the same dreams? How many times was the partner held in an embrace not the same as the partner held in fantasy and desire? And, Yeshua wondered, what did he himself really know of marriage, of its boredom and sometimes its violence? Often the reason for marrying is very different from the reason for staying married. Yeshua knew well the depths of the human heart, but how many truly happy marriages had he seen? How many love affairs that really last?

Perhaps he was counting them with his figures in the sand. Or was he simply thinking of the suffering of this woman who had given in to seduction? In the desert of her life, she had come upon a mirage of tenderness. . . .

Though Yeshua understood this woman, he also understood the point of view of Judas and the others. To them, marriage was sacred: In the union of man and woman, God is truly present. In every sacred union, God worked his creation, infusing the relationship and every part of the body with his joy. "Do not separate what the Lord has joined"—indeed, what love has joined, for God is love.

But what of those marriages into which God has not been truly invited, where the wine of love is absent? Are not such unions already nullified, if God has not been there to bless them?

Yeshua understood the thinking of the scribes and doctors of the Law: When love can no longer be felt in a marriage, it does not mean that love is really absent. There are degrees of asceticism; we do not remain faithful to others merely because we feel in love with them or because they satisfy our desire. We also remain faithful because we *want* to love them. This makes us capable of transcending our own pleasure to embrace the otherness of the Other. The childish love that is concerned only with the fulfillment of its own desires gives way to the adult love, which is capable of accepting its own longing and thinking more of the other's longing.

But adulterers are also a disturber of social harmony, for their act engenders desires for vengeance and crime, setting family against family. If allowed, it could destroy the unity of an entire nation. Thus it was understandable that some people felt it was better that two adulterers die rather than risk this destruction.

All of this Yeshua saw clearly. He did not judge any of them—scribe, Pharisee, or adulterer. He kept looking down at the ground, at the dust of which man and woman are made. Who had instilled such longings, such demands, into this dust?

Then he became totally silent, and listened to the voice of God within him. He was astonished at the notion that this same voice could be saying, simultaneously, to kill and not to kill all adulterers. Just as some marriages could be said to be merely a form of legalized prostitution, might there not be such a thing as legalized murder in a harsh and literal obedience to the commandments? Did not such interpretations provide a convenient escape from the bad conscience of human impulses toward violence and murder?

In this silence, Yeshua felt himself bow under the weight of this divine contradiction: "You shall not kill" and "Lead the impure ones to the gates of the city and stone them until they are dead. . . . Thus you shall rid yourselves of the evil amid you."

Yet he began to hear something else in these words, something that seemed to touch the heart of his own mission. There, where Judas heard "You will rid yourselves of fault, sin, and sinners"; there, where Judas saw a fault to be condemned, Yeshua perceived a misery that needed to be healed. He saw suffering and lowered his eyes in the face of this woman's sin. He wanted not to kill her, but to heal and deliver her from her sin, for "YHWH takes no pleasure in the death of a sinner. He desires that the sinner should live." The only way to be delivered of a desire is through a greater desire; we cannot free ourselves from a love except through a greater love.

Suddenly the adulteress herself could feel Yeshua's love for her. It was a love such as she had never known, whether from family or from lovers. She had been expecting to meet justice, and instead she was meeting compassion. She had been preparing herself for the justice of men, and now she was experiencing another kind of justice. Was it the justice of the God this man Yeshua carried within him?

Finally Judas could wait no more. "So, what do you think, Rabbi? The scribes are growing impatient. They are waiting for your answer and they expect you to confirm the Law of Moses and the punishment it prescribes. This will make them respect you as a righteous man. Just say one word, and she will die!"

Acquiescing to Judas's impatience, Yeshua stood up, and said:

"Let him who is without sin cast the first stone."*

> Let him who has never looked at a woman with lust cast the first stone.
> Let him who has never been unhappy, never thirsted for kindness, cast the first stone.
> Let him who has never been seduced by an illusion cast the first stone.
> Let him who has never deceived himself or others cast the first stone.
> Let him who is free of all desire, free of all doubt, and has never lied, cast the first stone.

With this one simple phrase, Yeshua compelled all who heard to look into their own hearts. Perhaps some of them realized that it was only fear or weakness that had prevented them from committing a crime punishable by death. How, then, could they judge others?

The Teacher was saying that one should use the Law as one uses a mirror: not to judge others, but to know oneself.

"Let him who is without sin cast the first stone."

With these simple and breathtaking words, Yeshua held a mirror up to all. Everyone there, the adulteress included, could see his own true face and the twisting paths of his own heart.

But when they heard him, they left, one by one, beginning with the eldest . . .†

Perhaps the eldest left first not because they had sinned more than

*John 8:7.

†John 8:9.

the others (though in some cases this might be true), but because, being closer to death, they had less taste for killing. The youngest men were reluctant to leave. If they did not stone this woman, they would be left to confront their own illicit desires with no violent act to exorcise them. They had yet to learn that it is love, far more than the threat of punishment, that could deliver them from the chains of passion.

These men still did not understand—yet they let the stones fall from their hands. And perhaps they felt a strange happiness at the touch of the breeze on their open palms.

Yeshua shook himself now, as if coming out of a trance. Certainly he was feeling happiness—after all, these men had been prevented from using the Torah as an excuse to add the crime of murder to that of adultery. Here, at least, no one had succeeded in invoking God so as to kill with a good conscience.

Now that the woman was delivered from her terror, Yeshua looked her calmly in the eyes for the first time. To her, it was as if his gaze washed over her like living waters. But these waters burned even as they cleansed. She had a vision of paradise and hell becoming one; this man's gaze would be unbearable for those who could not allow themselves to drown in it, and a balm for those who could.

> Woman, where have they gone? Has no one condemned you?*

Only this man could condemn her, for he alone could look into her eyes without a hint of lust or desire to please her or possess her. Yeshua's gaze seemed to her like that of a wondering child. "Have you ceased to suffer? Do you know now that the love you were seeking in outer experiences is within you, and that if you do not find it within you, you will never find it outside you? If you have this love in you, then nothing and no one can prevent you from loving, from being free.

---

*John 8:10.

You are capable of loving even your enemies, even your husband."

Go, and sin no more.*

In other words, from now on, never leave this source within you, never aim away from the goal of your life.†

Seek first the Kingdom, the reign of spirit within you, and "all the rest shall be added." Go and never turn back again! This is how you will make everything new.

Thus Yeshua was not inviting this woman into a new prison of guilt. His joy was to see her walk forth, straight ahead, with a new capacity of desire that took the place of her misguided desire. "Trust in God. The Master of the impossible will give you the strength to love each day. Go and be happy!"

For Judas, these final words of Yeshua to the woman were too much. And all this tender talk, dripping with honeyed words—once again, he felt the old nausea rising in his belly.

What had become of his Master, so full of fervor and power in the Temple as he drove out the unclean ones? Where were the harsh and burning words that he had previously found to chastise those who leave the way of righteousness? What was the source of this sudden weakness, this softness, this ridiculous sympathy for a woman condemned by the Law?

Now, Judas felt a sinister smile play upon his lips. "In any case," he thought with grim satisfaction, "your lovely words will change nothing. When the crowds begin to spit at you in the streets—men, women, and children—you will not be able to make them swallow back their saliva! The Law of YHWH condems this sort of pity, for it is nothing but complicity with evil."

---

*John 8:11. [These are Yeshua's final words to the adulteress. —*Trans.*]

†The meaning of the Greek word *hamartia,* a gospel word often translated as "sin," is actually "missing the mark," missing the goal.

# 12

# *Money*

In spite of the weakness that had overcome the Teacher when faced with the adulteress, Judas did not lose hope in him, for in Yeshua's company, a strange transformation would come upon him: Even the ugly features of his face seemed to relax and change and he became almost pleasant to look upon. He looked younger and acquired a dignity of bearing that exuded self-confidence. The other disciples noticed it, and he gained respect in their eyes.

One day Yeshua asked him to take responsibility as treasurer for the group and manage the donations of money they regularly received from those who had been moved by Yeshua's teaching. It was a difficult task, requiring the ability to write, calculate, and keep accounts. Matthew could easily have done it, with his experience as tax collector, but it would have reminded him too much of the life he had vowed to abandon.

Judas had shown great enthusiasm for Yeshua's teaching that we cannot serve two masters: both God and money. "Yes, we must not serve money, we must make money serve," Judas had added—a remark that gained everyone's approval. Thus it seemed natural that this important task be given to him.

But Judas had other plans as to how this money would "serve" not only to meet the material needs of the group, but also to purchase arms to prepare for the inevitable insurrection. Surely it would not be long before Yeshua, whom he still regarded as his Messiah-King, would finally have to announce it.

Yeshua showed little interest in financial matters. On the other hand, he often warned them about money and the reasons why it was so difficult for the rich to enter the Kingdom. If the mind and the heart are too preoccupied with money for its own sake, we become insensitive to others' needs. We are possessed by our own possessions. It is important to remain free. One of his favorite proverbs was "You will find your treasure where you find your heart."

Money is useful only when it helps us to find treasures more precious than money can buy. Money was intended as a means, a form of energy that must circulate—otherwise it will crush or burn us. To seek money for itself, as did that man on the road whose face lit up as he counted more and more of his coins, was for Yeshua a form of idolatry and thus of misery. That man had missed the true treasure, which can never be bought or counted: the light of peace in the heart.

But Judas considered Yeshua's attitude to be excessively spiritual and utopian. The Teacher seemed to lack a sound sense of worldly responsibilities. We are men—not birds or lilies of the field who neither reap nor sow! We must sow our fields, harvest them, and weave baskets to hold the fruits of our labor. Is it not written that man shall "live by the sweat of his brow"? Possessions acquired without work are ill-gained, a form of theft, and money itself was created to allow us to produce more and be more fruitful.

Yet there were other times when Yeshua's teaching seemed to agree strongly with Judas's notions:

For it will be as when a man going on a journey called his servants and entrusted to them his fortune: To one he gave five talents, to another two, to another one, to each according to his ability. Then he went away.

He who had received the five talents went at once and traded with them; and he made five talents more. So also, he who had the two talents made two talents more. But he who had received the one talent went and dug in the ground and hid his master's money.

Now, after a long time, the master of those servants came and settled accounts with them. And he who had received the five talents came forward, bringing five talents more and saying, "Master, you delivered to me five talents; here I have made five talents more."

His master said to him, "Well done, good and faithful servant; you have been faithful over a little, I will set you over much; enter into the joy of your master."

And he also who had the two talents came forward, saying, "Master, you delivered to me two talents; here I have made two talents more."

His master said to him, "Well done, good and faithful servant; you have been faithful over a little, I will set you over much; enter into the joy of your master."

He also who had received the one talent came forward, saying, "Master, I know you to be a hard bargainer, reaping where you did not sow, and gathering where you did not sift; so I was afraid, and I went and hid your talent in the ground. Here you have what is yours."

But his master answered him, "You wicked and slothful servant! I shall judge you by your own words! You knew that I reap where I have not sowed, and gather where I have not sifted? Then you ought to have invested my money with the bankers, and at my coming, I should have received what was my own with interest.

"So take the talent from him, and give it to him who has the ten talents. For to every one who has will more be given, and he will have abundance; but from him who has not, even what he has will be taken away.

"And cast the worthless servant into the outer darkness; there where there is weeping and gnashing of teeth."*

Here, Judas exulted in the real voice of the fierce Messiah he wanted to serve. This parable showed a strict demand, a harsh rejection of bad servants. This was the kind of Messiah Israel needed to become once again a flourishing nation governed by righteous and pure men.

But Yohanan had a different interpretation of the parable and tried to explain it to Judas: "What the master is asking of his servants is to use the money he has given them to bear more fruit and thereby earn as much as they have been given. The talents a servant is given represent his freedom. They have been given their freedom, which they can use to enter into the joy of their master. The servant who has not made use of his gift to produce anything is left with no more than he has been given. He has not grown or earned his freedom. Hence, he cannot enter into the joy of his master, and what he has held on to will be given to those who know how to make it bear fruit. This is why there is weeping and gnashing of teeth."

"Perhaps you are right, Yohanan. But do not worry about me—I will make my Master's money bear much fruit! What he has given us is the price of his teaching and his life. In our turn, we must transmit his teaching and add our own to it. Both his life and our lives must be given."

---

*Matthew 25:14–28,30.

Judas continued to exult at this teaching, but it was not long before he was faced with a new problem: the obligation to pay taxes to Caesar's collectors.

This prospect was totally unacceptable and unthinkable to him: "What? Give money to our oppressors so that they can find the means to oppress us even more? Give our money to pay for swords and arms for them to persecute us? No! This is money that we have gained by the sweat of our brows, walking through the dust of many roads and many towns. Rather use it to forge our own arms, which will free us from them!"

Yeshua said to him: "Bring me a coin." When it was brought, he asked: "Tell me, what is this effigy stamped upon the coin?"

"It is the effigy of Caesar," Judas answered.

"Then render unto Caesar what is Caesar's. And render unto God what is God's."*

Judas was hoping for further commentary in which Yeshua would add that because everything belongs to God, then Caesar must also be rendered unto God. If Caesar refused to submit to God, then they should refuse him not only taxes, but also any form of recognition or honor. But Yeshua was silent. Was this a teaching of a true Zealot or was it a teaching of compromise? Was he advocating submission of the body to the ruling authorities and submission of the heart to God? If so, was this not the same kind of hypocrisy and duplicity that Yeshua himself so often denounced? Or was it supposed to be some sort of diplomacy?

This only increased Judas's impatience. When would Yeshua finally manifest himself publicly to all? May the time of redemption come soon, for the salvation and liberation of Israel!

*Matthew 22:17–21.

# 13

## *Transfiguration*

Before the Shabbat began, Yeshua spoke to them.

"Truly, I tell you: There are some among you who will not taste death until they see the Kingdom of God."

Judas felt sure he was among those who would see the Law of God reborn to reign in Israel, so he was astonished when he was not among those invited by Yeshua to accompany him to the top of Mount Tabor. On that day, only Peter, Jacob, and Yohanan were chosen. Miriam was also among those who remained at the camp. Why was he going up there? There was surely no one to be taught or converted in that place. Probably he wished to "go up toward his Father" and pray. But why did he not go alone, as he usually did?

When Peter, Jacob, and Yohanan came down again, their eyes shone strangely, as if their faces had been washed by the light of a strange sun. Had Yeshua revealed a secret to them, a truth that the other disciples could not understand? "If Peter can understand, then even the dullest among us can," Judas muttered to himself. What had happened up there? The three were completely silent. Judas urged Miriam to try to find out. After all, she was close to Yohanan, and the latter was so trusting and naive that he would surely tell her.

Indeed, it was not long before Yohanan told her: "When we arrived at the summit, Yeshua went aside to pray. As he was praying, the whole nature of his face became transformed and his clothes were shining with a brilliant white light. And then two men appeared and spoke with him. They were none other than Moshe and Eliahu in their bodies of light! They spoke of the way that Yeshua must follow into Jerusalem. We were all three overcome by sleepiness, and when we awoke, this is what we saw: Yeshua, Moshe, and Eliahu in shining glory! Then Moshe and Eliahu disappeared. Peter said to Yeshua: 'Because we are here, let us set up three shelters, one for you, one for Moshe, and one for Eliahu.'*

"But as he was saying this, the shadow of a cloud came upon us and we were terrified. A voice came from the midst of this cloud, saying: 'This is My Son, the Beloved, the Chosen One. Listen to him.'†

"Then, it was all over. We found ourselves again, the three of us, alone with Yeshua. His body and his face had become ordinary again. Jacob prodded me in the ribs with his foot to show me that I was not dreaming. We decided not to speak of what we had seen—for who would believe us?

"What did he mean when he spoke of the Kingdom that some of us will see before death? I believe that YHWH, the I AM who was revealed to Moshe and Eliahu in their time, was manifested to us today! The body of Yeshua is our new burning bush, filled with the holy name, and the holy breath is the light breeze that surrounded the prophet. Surely he is the Chosen One, the Word of the Father addressed to us! It is he, the reign of YHWH among us!"

Miriam went to Judas and repeated to him Yohanan's words, then she added: "Now I understand why he did not invite me to climb Mount Tabor. I did not need to go there, for I have often

---

*Matthew 17:4.

†Matthew 17:5.

seen him transfigured in this way. The transfiguration that Yohanan, Peter, and Jacob saw on the mountain I have already contemplated from my own bed. I have seen Who Is in his fragile human body, I have felt the Invisible, the Infinite in my arms."

"That's enough, Miriam!" Judas yelled, clamping his strong, hairy hand over her mouth. "You are raving as Peter sometimes does! I, too, have often seen him transfigured, especially when he speaks. Does not the Divine, the Logos, speak through him? When he drove the money changers from the Temple, was it not the very incarnation of justice we witnessed? I, too, have seen his eyes shining like the sun. I have heard his voice resound like thunder. I have seen our Messiah storm in his glory, like the lightning that is soon to come when the impure will be consumed and the earth will tremble! What I have not yet seen is Moshe and Eliahu side by side with him. But never mind. The important thing is that this confirms what I already knew: It is he, Yeshua, who has come to fulfill the Law and the prophets!"

As they were speaking, some flowers had bloomed, covering the ground where they stood like white and red stars upon the ocher earth.

"Look, Judas!" Miriam exclaimed. "We have surprised the dust itself, breaking out into spring while we speak! Perhaps if our eyes were not so filled with dead stars, we would always see the earth transfigured in this way. . . . The holy light is always there, in the body of Yeshua, in the body of the earth. . . . It is our own blindness that prevents us from seeing it."

"Now you are speaking like a pagan!" Judas snapped. "You sound like a mediocre poet or a bad philosopher."

"But does not Yeshua himself urge us to contemplate the flowers of the fields and the birds of the sky? Do not the Wisdom and Love of YHWH manifest themselves in the least things of life, as witness to the Living One?"

"Very well, Miriam," Judas replied "continue to occupy yourself with the least things of life. But leave the great things to us men, the adults!"

"Yes," she replied, "and leave you to your wars! And leave us the lily and the jasmine! Leave to you the fire that destroys the land, and leave to us the flame that lights the hearth! Indeed, to be close to Yeshua is to be close to the fire . . . but whoever stands close to it will receive the kind of sparks for which he is looking."

"Women should be seen and not heard," Judas muttered, walking away.

No one ever got the last word with Miriam. It seemed that the only thing that could make her at a loss for words was the look or the kiss of her Teacher.

# 14

## *Encounter in the Desert*

After Mount Tabor, Yeshua seemed different. There were fewer miracles and no exorcisms. Sometimes his words seemed hesitant. To Judas, he seemed less like a prophet who spoke with conviction than a philosopher who asked questions.

"For you, who am I?" This question especially puzzled Judas: Does he no longer know who he is? Is he beginning to doubt his mission?

Judas suggested that Yeshua go spend some time in the desert in an effort to be closer to the voice and design of YHWH. It would only be fitting to act as all the great prophets before him and undertake a retreat of fasting and prayer before his entry into Jerusalem during Passover, when he would surely reveal himself as the long-awaited Messiah.

Yeshua accepted this suggestion, and the other disciples also felt it a good one. They all promised to fast and pray while he was gone so as to prepare for the great day that all sensed was coming.

Then Yeshua suggested that Judas accompany him—for the disciple, too needed to reflect on his own mission and needed to listen to the voice of YHWH and pray for the strength he would need to accomplish what must must be accomplished in Jerusalem.

Very soon, they set off together under the burning sun. Once they had arrived at a certain place in the desert, they separated, each toward his own cave. If YHWH granted them life, they vowed to meet here again after forty days and forty nights.

There came a morning when Yeshua did not sit still before the dawn, as he usually did, marveling at the almost unbearable beauty of the new day being born in the desert. This morning, his whole body ached. It was almost his fortieth day of solitude, silence, and fasting. He felt hungry—not only for food, but also for company. In spite of his weakness, he decided to take a walk.

After crossing over several dunes, he realized that he was not alone. A man was walking toward him or, more exactly, toward the well that was not far from the cave where he had taken refuge. Neither man spoke. Judas then gathered some sticks for kindling and lit a fire. It seemed he wanted to heat some water and share a beverage with Yeshua, as if he were an invited guest. He sat down and made a sign for Yeshua to do the same.

Yeshua regarded him silently for a while, then came and sat beside him. Far away in the desert, they saw a single silhouette formed from the two slopes of a hillock. One side was black, the other white, lit by the rising sun.

Looking at it, it was as if they silently recognized each other. Here they both were, led here by the Spirit to clarify what their mission really was, what sort of Messiah they would choose to incarnate. What God, what infinite Power, what infinite Presence must they manifest to the world so that all people might be saved and peace might finally come to all the nations?

Judas was the first to speak.

"If these stones could be transformed into bread for everyone, it would be enough. What more do men really want? With full bellies, there would be no more war. If all our material desires were satisfied, there would be no more rich or poor, no more injustice. What problems would be left to solve? What other blessings can we really long for if we can always savor and digest a good meal under a pleasant sky? Consider the animals, Yeshua. They start moving and searching only because they need food. Otherwise, they are content to sleep. What was the original Paradise if not trees that offer fruit and stones that offer bread? This is surely our mission as sons of God and true messiahs: to dissolve in a happy body and endless satisfaction all these vain desires that torment a person. What reality is there, outside of matter? This is where we will find the true God we must serve, the God who fills our bellies and delivers us from hunger."

Judas offered Yeshua a bowl that he had taken from his sack so that it could be filled with the water mixed with a few herbs that had just begun to boil. Yet in spite of feeling thirst, Yeshua gently declined. He explained that he had not completed his fast. Smiling, he added that the time was not far when they would raise their cups together, this time filled with wine.

Then, looking Judas in the eyes, he began to speak: "Man does not live by bread alone. A human being is more than a belly to be filled, more than a material body. We have other hungers: for friendship, poetry, beauty, truth. Do not believe our desires can be reduced to our most basic needs. Satisfaction is not happiness. Just look at the richest and greatest among us—have you looked in their eyes? They lack nothing materially, yet they lack the essential. A human being is not fed by food alone, but also by true silence, by words of truth and light. And within a human being there is also an infinite desire that only Infinity can satisfy. This is the Messiah for which they are truly waiting: someone who knows and listens to the most secret desire of all, the desire that is hidden in the midst of all these other hungers. All human beings desire YHWH, the

One Who Is, from whom they came, and to whom they return."

"But Yeshua," Judas objected, "just try preaching these same words to men with empty stomachs sometime—they will spit in your face! We come from earth and we return to earth. This is all there is, and our responsibility is to make this world happy. You will only poison the lives of the poor and wretched by trying to convince them that they really want something else—silence, love, and light! Look at the beauty of that blue sky—yet you will find nothing to eat there! Let us be more realistic, Yeshua. Let us not promise people what is impossible."

"I am not a fool, Judas. I know well that we cannot speak of God to someone with an empty stomach in the same way we do to someone with a full one. We must increase and distribute the bread so that all receive their share. Yet a human being is more than this need. Offer them bread, by all means, but offer them also your hand. Offer them clothes to keep them warm, but offer them also the warmth of your presence. Give them words of knowledge, but give them also the silence and clarity of your eyes. Nourish and caress them, but do not forget to open their hearts, to light up their minds."

Judas only shrugged at this and sighed. "Poor Messiah, gentle dreamer," he thought. "As for me, I must concentrate on a task more tangible and useful than yours."

For a long time the two men remained sitting, each lost in his own reflections.

Suddenly Judas stood up and faced Yeshua: "For the sake of YWHW, our God, Yeshua! What we must do is bring all nations together and unite them as one! Under the banner of one leader, one master of the world, all must submit to God! That is the only real solution. As long as we have differences among nations, cultures, languages, races, and religions, we will never live in the image of God, for God is One. This is the Messiah the whole world is waiting for: someone who can teach all human beings what is right and wrong, that there is only one Law for us all! Obviously, in the early stages, force will be needed to bring this about. But when all have been brought into obedience to only one central power in all the world, we will all have peace, harmony, and agreement among us once again. Men must be forced into happiness, Yeshua, they must walk to the same rhythm, in the same direction."

Now Judas made great gestures, speaking ecstatically. "May the Kingdom of God come, may his Name be imposed upon all men! Away with the infidels, the ungodly, the impure, so that justice be accomplished! There is no other solution, Yeshua! A single God, a single Messiah, and a single power: Let us bow before the single God, Yeshua! Let us incarnate God, for there is no other reality, no other God."

While Judas stood thus before him, raving and glowing in his euphoric certainty, Yeshua turned away his gaze, looking at the far horizon. It was as if he was searching for an invisible oasis there.

When Judas became calmer, Yeshua spoke quietly. "Your single God is not God, Judas; it is an idol—an idol of power and an ideology. We do not say God is single—we say God is One. The One respects multiplicity and differences, but the single destroys them. Life takes on many different faces, totally different kinds of bodies, and yet life is One. We breathe the same air, yet we each breathe in our own fashion. It is true that we human beings are much alike, for we have the same kind of skeleton and bodily structure—you want to reduce human beings to that. But what I love in human beings is that which surrounds and animates the skeleton. The skulls of the dead look much alike, but look at living faces—is their beauty not in their differences from each other? Why do you want us to live in a single world? Do you want to see a single face, a single color of skin everywhere? And a single God—or rather, a single idol! Is not our task the opposite of this, to save humanity from uniformity, from being reduced to serving a single power imposed upon them?"

"Our God," Judas replied, "is called the Almighty, and it is through might that he shall impose himself upon all. Otherwise, there can never be peace or unity among peoples. The Messiah we wait for must have this might within him."

"You cannot force people to be happy. To attempt to do so is to deny their freedom. You cannot obligate people to love—that can only prevent them from loving and from discovering the One that unites them yet also allows them to be different."

"What are you saying, Yeshua? Is not our religion the only true one? If it is, then it must be obligatory for all, for there is no other way to unite the world. Are you denying that the religion of our fathers is the only true one and that all must submit to its Law?"

"The desert has invaded you, Judas. Every grain of sand may look just like all the others, yet if you look closely, each is different. Think of the water that makes a garden live; the same water makes roses flower red, lilies flower white, and all the other blooms flower in their own colors. Is not the beauty of a bouquet due to the harmony and contrast of different flowers? Thus we human beings offer up to God a bouquet composed of different praises. The very differences in our religions should stimulate us to go farther toward the one Good. Our differences in languages, races, and cultures are a celebration of the infinite variety of one life.

"And if, as you say, we must use the power of the Almighty within us, that power can manifest only as love. Only love can empower us to make our differences into a blessing rather than oppositions and exclusions. But this will never come about by mixing everything together, using force to make everything uniform or reducing everything to a common denominator. No, Judas, I will not bow to a God other than the God of love. Love is the only aspect of God that cannot be made into an idol, for love can be sustained only through giving it away. Did not our prophet Isaiah use the word *servant* to describe the coming Messiah?"

"A servant!" Judas exclaimed. "What? A Messiah who serves the orders of the rich and powerful? Is your Messiah to be a dog who cringes before the masters of this world? I pity you, Yeshua!"

"No, Judas. Not a dog who cringes. And in any case, is not a live dog who warns of danger and serves his master better than a dead lion? No, not a dog, Judas, but a man—a man who loves dogs and humans, plants and stars, and allows them all to be different. A man with wisdom, who knows how to savor the taste of the One in the heart of multiplicity."

"Yeshua, now you are talking as one of those philosophers does. All this chatter makes me begin to doubt that you are the one we have been waiting for. I will not bow before the arguments of your marvelous reasoning! I will bow only before a single Power, the Universal, not all these particulars. It is he alone I worship."

"Judas, you are like the outlaw in the story, the one who put into his bed everyone he captured. If they were too tall, he cut off their feet. If they were too short, he stretched them on a rack. He made them all the same size. When everyone is forced to be equal, no one is happy, no one is authentic. The real question is this: Without using force, how can we allow all to be who they are? Imagine a world without borders, with cities where there are common shelters instead of walls. . . . "

"Imagination is not enough, Yeshua! If we want a world without borders, we must force men to destroy them, to break down the walls. And for this, they must be obliged to speak a single language. Peace can be had only by imposing it on people. You speak of humans as if they are basically adult, free, and responsible beings—you're dreaming! Just look at the history of our own people and of other peoples as well: People are terrible! They behave as unruly children, children who have been indulged with too much affection so that they become like wild, stupid animals. And just as with animals, it is only through the whip that children or adults become gentle and humble."

"I disagree with you, Judas. Evil is not cured through evil, nor violence through violence. Thorns do not grow into grapes. A tree is known by its fruits. How can you imagine that love will be born from hatred or peace from war?"

"I simply look at history. And I advise you to do the same," Judas retorted.

Yeshua stood in silence. Then Judas walked over to the well and looked down into it. Turning to Yeshua, he said: "A true Son of God would never be afraid to jump into this well. He would know that God is with him and that God's angels will keep any harm from coming to him. He could even throw himself from the pinnacle of the Temple of Jerusalem without breaking a single bone. This is the kind of Messiah we are waiting for, Yeshua! Someone who will awe and subjugate the people by the power and magic of God in him. No one could doubt that he was the Messiah, for he would be the living proof of the existence and power of God."

"No, Judas," Yeshua replied. "He would be the living proof of the existence of a power that pretends to be God. Your Messiah is a mere magician, a miracle worker. Such a Messiah is a usurper."

"Call it what you like, Yeshua—it is what we need. What people need most is to be delivered from the torment of doubt. People need to be entranced, seduced, and compelled. What sort of Messiah would leave room for even the slightest doubt? The only true Messiah is one who blinds us with the light of proof!"

"Judas, a Messiah who loves human freedom would never force human beings either to love or to believe."

"Yeshua, what sort of God do you believe in—one who does not want us to have full stomachs? One who does not want our world united under one power? A God who will never use any means to seduce or force us to do anything? Why have you come to the desert for this retreat if not to develop your own powers? If you would only say yes to your power, you would be the greatest leader, obeyed by all, with a clear vision for all nations. No one could stand against you! And if any were unable to see that you want their happiness and salvation, you could convince them with beautiful miracles. They would fall to the ground and worship you."

Now Yeshua and Judas approached each other slowly. Both of them showed fatigue, as if acknowledging the futility of their debate, for it was clear that each was convinced of his position and neither was going to change it. As they drew near, Yeshua gave Judas a kiss, saying gently: "We will see each other later, my friend. Now let us go pray." Each retired to his place. Only the desert wind and a moving serpent were witnesses as they prayed.

Yeshua's beautiful voice rose up in a chant:

*A'woon dwash'maya*
*Nethkadash shmakh*
*Tethey mal'kuthakh*
*Neweh sewe'yanakh*
*A'kana dwash'maya*
*Ap bar'ah*
*Haw' lan 'lahma*
*Sun'kanan yau'mana*
*Washwok 'lan 'haw 'bain*
*Akana dap h'nan*
*'Shwakan l'hayawen*
*W'la'taalan (l') 'hysiona*
*Ella pasan min-bisha*
*Mitol ddee'la khee*
*Malkuthakh (w') tlaila (w') tizota*

*La 'alam almeen*
*Amen.*

Our Father who is in heaven,
may your Name be sacred,
may your Kingdom come,
may your Will be done,
on earth as in heaven.
Give us this day
our essential food.
Forgive us our offenses
as we forgive those who offend us.
Let us not be carried away
by trials;
deliver us from delusion,
for to you belong
the Kingdom, the Power, and the Glory.

But now, another voice was heard chanting, not far away. It was a beautiful bass voice, but tense and grandiose.

God of all powers,
Master of all worlds,
May Your Name
Make all nations tremble and submit.
May Your Kingdom be imposed upon all.
May none oppose Your Will,
Neither in heaven, nor on earth,
Nor in any of the worlds between.
Give us the bread and abundance
That all humans need.

May there be no pity, no pardon, for the ungodly.
Through our trials,
Make us strong and victorious.
Deliver us from weakness.
Show us the way to our goal
By any means,
For to You belong
The Kingdom, the Power, and the Glory . . .

# 15

## *Jerusalem*

From this time on, the disagreement between Yeshua and Judas was very clear. Yet in spite of the radical difference in their prayers and in their visions of the Messiah, they returned from the desert together as friends. Strangely, their friendship seemed to have deepened.

Judas had also acquired a certain authority among the other disciples. When he announced to them that Yeshua was going to make a triumphal entry into Jerusalem, where all would recognize him as the Messiah, they did not doubt him.

"Let us go and prepare the entry of the new King of Israel into the holy city!" he told them. "The Master has said that we will find a mother donkey with her foal nearby, tethered next to the Mount of Olives. Go there and take them," he ordered. "If anyone questions you, tell him the Messiah needs them!"

Judas also told the disciples that everything would come to pass as foretold by the prophet Zechariah:

Rejoice greatly, O daughter of Zion! Shout aloud, O daughter of

Jerusalem! Lo, your king comes to you, triumphant and victorious, yet humble and riding on a donkey, on a colt, the foal of a donkey.*

The disciples went to Bethphage, near the Mount of Olives. There, they found the donkeys and led them to Yeshua. They spread cloths over the animals' backs and asked Yeshua to mount one of them. Judas was explaining that the Messiah must be mounted on a donkey not only to fulfill the scriptures, but also because the long ears of this animal symbolize attention, for the time had come for all Israel to listen to its Messiah-King. Had the Law not had been given to the Jews with the words *shema, Yisrael,* "Listen Israel"?

"Now, all of you run through the streets of the city," Judas commanded, "and cry out, loud and strong, that the Messiah has arrived and that all must come and honor him!"

Soon a large crowd had gathered. They brought many palm branches as well as many cloths to cover the way where Yeshua was passing, mounted on the donkey. The disciples invited men, women, and children to chant loudly with them:

Hosanna, to the son of David!
Blessed is he who comes in the name of Adonai,
Hosanna to the highest heavens!†

Hearing these cries, the people of Jerusalem began to wonder and ask: "Who is this man?" And the crowd replied in unison: "He is the Messiah, the prophet Yeshua from Nazareth in Galilee!"

Judas was filled with exultation. Now the great day was surely at hand! Yeshua was shown what immense crowds he could draw.

---

*Zechariah 9:9.

†Matthew 21:9.

Judas had paid the money for the arms they would need. All he had to do was say the word to the Zealots who were waiting in Jerusalem and the insurrection would begin. The Romans would quickly be routed and the Sadducee high priests and minions of Herod would be forced to surrender. Yeshua would then mount the throne and the lineage of David would finally reign once more in Israel!

But it seemed that for Yeshua, things were not so simple. His attitude was strange and cryptic. When some citizens came out from the gates of Jerusalem to complain that his disciples were too noisy, he said: "I tell you, if they fall silent, the stones will cry out." Well, whatever that meant, at least it showed he approved of this noisy scene, which Judas was convinced would make the authorities tremble and would destabilize them.

Yet Yeshua's features were not joyous like those of his disciples. Miriam even detected a certain sadness in his eyes. A sad Messiah! How was such a thing possible?

Now she experienced a kind of premonition of the danger at hand. This kind of popular excess was bound to stir up the jealousy and wrath of the Sadducee high priests, the Pharisees, and others of the religious establishment. They were bound to react and plot to do away with Yeshua. It was known that they often resorted to poisons, which are quieter and deadlier than arms, so she vowed to redouble her vigilance in overseeing everything that was prepared for the Teacher to eat or drink.

But Miriam had another heavy weight on her mind: Her brother Lazarus was seriously ill and had hoped Yeshua would visit him. But the Teacher had seemingly had no time for a detour to visit Bethany and his "second family," as people called them, where he liked to go and rest with his friends.

The huge, festive crowd accompanied Yeshua to the gates of Jerusalem. All were waiting there for a speech—but he said nothing and withdrew.

It was Judas who first overcame his astonishment and made a hasty speech, reassuring the crowd that the Messiah needed a little rest, after which he would return to show them the way to follow so that their dreams would finally become reality and their joy would be complete.

Yeshua had gone to climb a small hill not far from the city walls. From this spot he had a good view of Jerusalem. Seeing the Temple, he began to weep, addressing it:

> Ah, if only today you knew the things that bring about peace! But they remain hidden from your eyes. For the days shall come when your enemies will erect a mass around you, surrounding you and hemming you in on every side; and they will batter you to the ground, you and your children within you, and they will not leave one stone standing upon another inside you. For you did not recognize my passage in your midst.*

As Judas approached Yeshua, he noticed the tears. This was so intolerable a sight to him that he seized Yeshua by the shoulders and shook him, looking him in the eyes: "What has come over you? The crowd is acclaiming you with great joy and you weep! Is this how you plan to liberate and save your people? Leave the tears to Miriam and all the other women who slow the pace of our triumphal march! Yeshua, your hour has come! Do not let dark thoughts cover your heart now! Rejoice, Son of Adonai, and stand proudly! Victory is at hand!"

Then Judas paused. In a quiet but firm voice, he began to speak: "Lazarus is almost dead. Let him remain in the tomb for three or

---

*Luke 19:44.

four days, then go and resurrect him. We will make sure there are many witnesses. This is the miracle we need. It will win to our cause even the most reticent. You know that what I told you in the desert is true: People need signs and wonders. They want to be compelled to believe. And they will believe in you! Afterward, we can do as we want with them—and what you and I want is the same thing: that the Kingdom of God arrive! It will arrive with your reign! It is too late to turn back now, Yeshua."

# 16

## *Lazarus*

Miriam dearly loved her brother Lazarus. When she was very young, he had awakened her to a love for the Torah and had taught her to read and study it. Unfortunately, this became just another reason for people to call her a sinner, for was not such study reserved for men? A woman who studied the Torah was regarded as an outlaw.

But Rabbi Yeshua disagreed with this view, and she soon became his favorite disciple and his intimate companion, to the amazement of the other disciples, especially Judas. Miriam also introduced Lazarus and her sister Martha to Yeshua. This was how Bethany became a sort of refuge for him, not only because of Miriam, but also because of the many deep discussions he had with Lazarus about different interpretations of the Torah and the implication of freedom that YHWH offers to those who will accept it. Every verse of the Torah, like every event of our life, is open to our interpretation. Nothing is pure or impure in itself; everything depends on what we make of it.

Sometimes their conversations lasted far into the night. Martha and the other disciples invited by Miriam listened with admiration to these discussions, but it was sometimes mixed with frustration at all the subtleties seemingly hidden in every letter of the Book. Once Lazarus said, "Intelligence alone cannot rediscover the Spirit, the Breath that inspired these letters—we must also read with our heart." Yeshua greatly approved of this.

Though Lazarus was a close friend of Yeshua, he never formally became a disciple. Lazarus said that the teaching of Rabbi Hillel of Shammaï was sufficient for him. And besides, he could see no essential difference between the two men's teachings, except for one aspect: that outlandish, impossible commandment of Yeshua's to love your enemies. But the rest of Yeshua's teachings seemed very sound to Lazarus and in accord with the authentic teaching of the Pharisees.

Yet he had to admit that Miriam had a point when she said with a smile: "But the difference is that he practices the teaching. He gives his very flesh and bones to the Torah."

Judas never cared much for Lazarus. He smelled of parchment; he was a rich bookworm cared for by his devoted sister Martha. What did a man like that know of the suffering of the poor under the Roman boot? Judas could not understand what Yeshua saw in him. It must be Miriam's influence.

Judas had already informed Yeshua of Lazarus's condition, so there was little surprise when his death was announced soon afterward. Yeshua stayed another two days in the same place, and then announced to his disciples: "Come with me. Our friend Lazarus is asleep and I go to awaken him. Lazarus has died, and I am glad I was not there at the time, so that you should believe."

Judas was overjoyed upon hearing these words. Yeshua was finally beginning to understand!

On the road, they meet Martha, who spoke to Yeshua: "Rabbi, if you had been there, my brother would not be dead. But even now, I know that YHWH will answer your prayers."

"Your brother will rise again," Yeshua answered.

"I know that—for I believe in the resurrection on the Last Day."

"I AM the resurrection. The 'I AM' is the resurrection and the life. Whoever believes in I AM lives, even if he dies. Whoever lives and believes in I AM can never die. Do you believe that?"

"Yes. And I believe that you are the Messiah, the son of the Most High, the one who has come into the world."*

Judas was profoundly impressed by the power of these words of the Teacher, and took them to heart. They meant that whoever, like Yeshua, discovered within themselves the presence of I AM, or YHWH, would never die, for they were already resurrected. "Then Yeshua is already resurrected . . . and I, too, am resurrected! What does it matter if we die? The only thing that has died is our fear of death, our attachment to our mortal nature. We go, we return to where I AM has always been. We find our true nature, our heaven and earth, the land we should never have left, the land we forgot. . . . Probably Martha understands nothing of this, yet she believes. Through her faith, she can be in touch with the I AM in herself, as in Yeshua, that cannot die."

But his meditations were interrupted by the sound of Miriam's sobbing. To her, her brother was quite dead, for he had been in the tomb for almost four days.

Then Judas noticed that Yeshua's eyes were also full of tears. "What a strange Messiah this is! Only moments ago, he had a God-like serenity and authority as he affirmed the I AM of YHWH in himself as the resurrection and the Life, and affirmed that Lazarus had no reason to fear death. And now he is crying, just like an ordinary man crying over the death of a friend!"

---

*John 11:1–27.

He then asked his Teacher: "What is the matter, Yeshua? Are you having doubts about this *anastasis,* this resurrection in which you want us to believe?"

It was Philip who answered him. "But Judas, we are still human beings, here on earth. There is no shame in crying for a friend. Yeshua is certainly divine, but he is also human—all the more human: divinely human."

Yeshua had heard Judas, just as he had recently heard some Jews who had witnessed all this and who said: "See how much he loved his friend? But why did not this man, who opened the eyes of the blind, prevent his friend from dying?"

After a pause, Yeshua commanded: "Move the stone away from the tomb."

Martha was upset: "But Master, this is the fourth day; the corpse will already be decaying. . . ."

Yeshua replied: "Have I not told you that if you believe, you will see the glory of YHWH?"

While the stone was being removed, Yeshua prayed:

Abba, I render You grace,
I know that You are listening to me,
It is because of this crowd surrounding me
That am speaking and acting,
So that they will believe that You have sent me.*

Then Yeshua cried out in a loud voice: "Lazarus, come forth!"

A figure emerged from the tomb, covered with bandages and the shroud over his face. All watching were aghast, scarcely believing their eyes. But Yeshua spoke calmly and ordered them: "Untie him and let him go."

---

*John 11:41–42.

Judas was beside himself with joy. He began to shout: "Yeshua is master of life and death! He has resurrected Lazarus and he will reawaken us all, whatever the death that has us in its grip! Let us shake off our shrouds, untie the bandages that keep us bound to the dust, and walk with him, for he is our Savior!"

There were many high-ranking Judaeans who knew Lazarus and his family and had come to mourn him. Seeing this, they believed in Yeshua.

Some of them told the high priests what they had witnessed. The latter, alarmed by this, held a special council. "What shall we do? This man has worked amazing miracles. If we allow him to continue, everyone will believe in him. They will proclaim him king, and this will infuriate the Romans, for they will allow no king other than Caesar. They will then destroy our holy Temple and our nation."

Caiaphas, who was the high priest that year, said: "It is better for one man to die than for a whole people to die." This convinced them, and they decided that Yeshua must die.

Judas had a close informant who was a servant of the high priest. When he learned of this decision, he acted quickly, taking money from the communal funds to buy more arms. Now those whom he was starting to refer to as "the partisans of the Messiah" would have the means to defend Yeshua and destroy those who threatened his life.

# 17

## *Bethany*

As Passover drew near, great numbers of people arrived in Jerusalem from the surrounding countryside. They had heard of Yeshua and were asking after him, wondering if he would be at the Passover festival. There were rumors of the dangers threatening him, and many had already declared themselves ready to defend him. Who could doubt him after all these signs and miracles? He could surely crush his opponents, if he chose.

But Yeshua kept out of sight as he prepared for Passover with his friends at Bethany. Lazarus was there and had described his experience during the four days when he was dead. He spoke of a strange voyage through intermediary worlds between body and spirit, and of all the "climates" he had to traverse before rejoining the pure light. All of these worlds were composed of the records of his actions, thoughts, emotions, feelings, perceptions, and desires during his entire mortal existence.

Miriam took careful note of her brother's account. Like Judas, she felt a desire to write down her version of the good news some day, and to tell what she had experienced with her Rabbouni, her beloved Teacher.

Yeshua was surprised at the amount of detail in Lazarus's account. He had thought his friend's access to the pure light would have been simpler. Lazarus wondered how Yeshua had been able to induce his soul to return to the lifeless body and reanimate it. Yeshua answered that Lazarus's soul had not gone very far. It had not gone so far as to lose all its attachment to the mortal body. This also explained the nature of what he had experienced in the intermediary worlds, where the soul is purified before becoming one with Spirit.

But this was no time for such discussions. A sense of danger filled the atmosphere all around the house at Bethany, and some even imagined Roman soldiers suddenly appearing to arrest the one denounced by the high priests, the troublemaker and usurper of Caesar's throne. For now, however, Yeshua was safe here.

Miriam was even more worried than the others. She had a growing premonition of what was about to happen, but had no words to describe it. It seemed that all she had as a means of expression were her hands, her mute lips, and her hair—indeed, her whole body trembled with it.

She went into her room and returned with an alabaster jar filled with a very pure and costly essential oil. She kneeled before Yeshua and solemnly poured the perfumed oil upon his feet, as if performing a ceremony of anointment. Then she massaged his feet gently with her expert hands. Finally, she dried his feet with her long hair. The house was filled with the exquisite perfume of the oil.

The disciples were used to Miriam's extravagances, but this seemed beyond all reason. Such oil must cost a fortune! Yet her gestures were those of an ancient pagan priestess, a ritual anointment of the king who must die. . . . After all, did not the Hebrew word *mashiakh* literally mean "the anointed one"? In this moment, did not Miriam wordlessly recognize her beloved as the Messiah, the young king who must die? Her head and her heart were surely filled with trouble and confusion, but were not her actions perfect in their graceful symbolism?

But most of the disciples did not see this. Judas, especially, was offended, for he knew the price of such an oil. "This expensive oil you have used could have been sold for three hundred pieces of silver—enough to feed many hungry people!" he admonished her. In reality, he was thinking about the arms he could have bought.

The disciples mostly supported Judas in this, but Yeshua intervened: "Leave her in peace. She has been keeping this precious oil for the day of my burial. But why wait until someone is dead to offer him flowers, perfumed oil, or tears? Is it not better to offer intimate gifts while a person is alive? Unfortunately, the poor and the miserable will still be with you after I am gone. Take care of even the least of them as you would my own body; it is the I AM for which you are caring. Do not deny yourself this generosity, for it is through the gift of yourself that you will become divine. Yes, the poor will long be with you—but I will not as I am today. Miriam already knows this. You, too, must know it: I shall never grow old, for I am going to die."

"No, you are not going to die!" Judas objected.

"You possess the words of life eternal," Peter added.

"And why should I not die?" Yeshua asked. "Am I not a human being, like you, created from dust and bound to return to dust?"

"Created from Light!" Yohanan exclaimed.

"You are right, Yohanan," Yeshua replied, "but the night is never far from the day. . . ."

Once more, Judas found himself surprised and disgusted by Yeshua's words and behavior. Bewailing his approaching death, allowing this woman to wash his feet with such expensive oil, sitting back and savoring its perfume—was this any way to raise the morale of his troops, who were ready to die to protect him?

Judas left hastily, for he wanted to reflect and not to betray his anger to the others. Was not Yeshua betraying him, the most faithful of his disciples, by taking Miriam's side in this matter? Agreeing with a woman against a man ready to gather an army to protect him—was this not a sign of betrayal? Was it not even a sign of dangerous treachery, which risked compromising the coming of the reign of YHWH and his Messiah? Judas was beginning to feel a sense of profound disappointment in exact proportion to the loftiness of his hopes, his boundless expectations projected upon Yeshua. Boundless? Indeed—boundless, just like the boundless expectations of the people of Israel. And if these expectations were disappointed, then that disappointment would be boundless as well.

Now Judas was shaken deeply, torn by opposite emotions clashing and coursing through his body, mind, and soul. A disappointed man is a dangerous man, for he who believes he has been betrayed becomes capable of betrayal. For the first time, doubt and even hatred began to infiltrate his faith and admiration of Yeshua—but he shook this off violently and recovered himself quickly. "Now I see—Yeshua is testing us! He is showing us his weakest, most human side to force us to react and then make him react so that he will unveil the Divinity and Power within him! It is through such tests that the Messiah makes our faith firmer and our hope firmer."

# 18

## *An Unexpected Messiah*

The Messiah who comes may not be the one expected. Judas found that he was less and less able to make Yeshua fit his image of the Messenger of God. His behavior with women, his absurd philosophizing in the desert, his tears over Jerusalem, his softness in dealing with the adulteress—and now this incident at Bethany: It was becoming too much, and Judas's deep trouble would not leave him. He kept coming back to Yohanan the Baptist's question: Is he the one we for whom we have been waiting? "Might it not be another?" Judas wondered. "Or perhaps no one? . . . Perhaps I should stop waiting for the Messiah and count on my own strength and our force of arms to drive out the Roman occupier. Why not develop my own potential instead of looking for it in someone else?" Judas even began to wonder if he himself could be the real Messiah that he had been hoping to find in Yeshua.

But even as he rejected such thoughts, he remembered something Yohanan had said to him one day: "Never have I seen anything so beautiful, so true, so good as Yeshua. Our heart is made for an infinite love, and Yeshua is the only human being I have ever encountered who is capable of receiving this infinite love. What other creature or object on earth or in the sky could I love more than him? Who else could be so worthy of my faith? If some philosopher offered me a proof that Yeshua was not the incarnation of truth and justice, I would still choose Yeshua—and leave the philosopher to his abstractions of truth and justice!" But Judas balked at this last part. If he, Judas, had to choose, it would be for truth and justice over Yeshua.

Judas continued to mull over such thoughts as he made his way toward the room high up on Mount Zion, where Yeshua and the others were waiting to celebrate the Passover.

When they were all sitting at the table, Yeshua silently stood up, took a towel and a basin of water, and then began to kneel before each disciple in turn, washing and drying his feet. When he came to Peter, the disciple said: "Master, it is not you who should be washing my feet!"

Yeshua answered: "This that I do, you do not yet understand. Later, you will."

"But I cannot allow *you* to wash *my* feet!"

"If I do not wash them, you will not be with the I AM."

"Oh, Master, then you must wash my head and my hands as well."

"Whoever has been baptized does not need to bathe in this place. He is pure already, and you have all been purified by the word you have heard. You are not all entirely pure, however."

Now Yeshua came to Judas, and was silent.

Judas's head was racing with thoughts. "Yeshua is going mad! He is acting just as Miriam acts! Will he also dry our feet with his hair? If so, he may as well lick them, as a dog or a prostitute would!" He felt as if he wanted to protest, as Peter had, but said instead: "No, do not touch me in this way; do not wash my feet! Stand up, Yeshua, and behave as the Master you are! The Messiah's place is not at our feet! You should be walking nobly and erect, like a god—and we should be following in your footsteps."

When Judas felt the water flow over his feet, he began to shake with anger. For the first time, he wanted to slap Yeshua in the face. His dream was crumbling before his eyes. How could he put his trust in someone smaller than himself, someone behaving as a mere servant? Yeshua was a slave dressed in the clothes of a master. He was an ignorant but skillful actor, imitating the words of a real Teacher! Lazarus was so right when he said that Hillel was sufficient for him—in fact, Yeshua was a weakling, an impotent fraud.

Now Judas began to laugh. How manipulated he had been! How could he have not seen through this ridiculous messiah, acting so much as a woman in love, kneeling at his feet in this way?

The other disciples interpreted his laughter as an expression of pleasure and good humor. But Yeshua clearly perceived the rage, sadness, disappointment, and distress hidden in it. Judas remained so alienated from the power of love. He worshipped power, nobility, courage—for him, love was mostly a mask for weakness and cowardice. For him, God was the Almighty, Master of the Universe. He could not be a God of love, for that would render him powerless before those who resisted him. Was Yeshua the Messiah of that God?

For any force, an opposing force may be found. But what is the opposing force of love? Refusal, no doubt, or attraction to nothingness; but even in these cases, did not love emerge the victor? If anger, rage, and condemnation are the strengths of the weak, then kindness and forgiveness are the strengths of the strong. Love cannot look upon us from above; it wants to kneel at our feet, not to fawn upon us or lower itself, but to heal our wounded feet, the lowest parts of our bodies, to help us stand and walk again.

This was the God incarnated by Yeshua, but Judas wanted nothing to do with such a God. Rather, he could not even recognize such a God because he was blinded by his ideal of God. He was entranced by the image of an all-powerful Messiah, an image that had been forged over the centuries. How could the true Yeshua compete with such a grandiose image?

When Yeshua had finished washing the feet of all the disciples, he returned to the table and spoke.

"Do you understand what I have just done? You do well to call me Master, Teacher, and Lord, for you are speaking to the I AM. If the Lord has washed your feet, then you too should wash the feet of others. I have given you this as an example so that you may do for others what I have done for you. Truly, truly, I tell you: The servant is not greater than his master, nor is the messenger greater than he who sends him. Knowing this, you will be happy if you do this yourselves . . ."

"No!" Judas interrupted, leaping to his feat and shouting. "Woe upon us all! Yeshua is founding a religion of slaves. If we do what he says, the powerful will continue to walk all over us, the Romans will always oppress us! Now you hear his real message: He is preaching surrender, resignation, capitulation, just as a traitor does! And we who listen to him, did we not hope that he would bring justice? But now he advocates collaboration with the unjust—he wants us to lick their boots, wash their feet. He is a traitor!"

For a moment, a scandalous notion occurred to Judas: Because everything was lost and nothing more could be expected of this coward, this false messiah who had misled them, destroying all their hopes and expectations, why not just deliver him to the priests who wanted to do away with him? That way, Yeshua would get what he was looking for, and his abdication would receive the punishment it deserved.

But now the other Judas took over, the one who continued desperately to believe in Yeshua as the Messiah: "No! If he is taken by the soldiers, it will only force him to awaken! YHWH, the Almighty, will manifest in him once more, and help him to accomplish greater miracles—greater, even, than the resurrection of Lazarus, greater than the healing of the blind man, the paralytic, or any of the others! Surely he who had been able to drive away all these demons would show himself capable of driving away the Romans! And even if they do kill him . . . I am certain, I truly believe, that he would be able to resurrect himself and emerge from the tomb. That would be a manifestation of power that all would be compelled to recognize—for Yeshua is indeed the Messiah of Israel, the Son of Our Heavenly Father. After all, doesn't he call him 'Abba'? He needs only to be awakened."

At this point his glance met Yeshua's eyes. He felt as if a sword had pierced his heart. A strange heat invaded Judas and tears shone in his eyes—even in this man with those eyes of stone.

And finally, Judas understood everything.

The Master was *asking* him to deliver him to the priests! This would force the hand of the occupiers, for they would crucify him as a common criminal, and then he would be resurrected and demonstrate to the world his power over death! "Only death dies," Yeshua had said once in discussion with Lazarus. "I AM is eternal; it cannot die, it will be with us through the end of the world."

Yeshua continued to fix Judas with his gaze. Such incredible kindness and strength were revealed there, such friendship and trust . . . Judas lowered his eyes in embarassment. He thought, "Who am I for him to entrust me with such an awesome mission?" But Judas already felt the sense of ascendancy that comes with surrender to a greater being. He saw the profound truth of humility and the nobility of this service offered to him—a service that would remain unknown and misunderstood by everyone.

In this moment, Judas felt closer to Yeshua than ever before. He was ashamed of the negative, bitter thoughts he had entertained about his Master and of his delusions as to the nature of the hard struggle before him. He now understood what he must do "so that the scriptures may be fulfilled." He looked again at Yeshua and made a slight nod of understanding and acceptance. He had a desire to embrace Yeshua, but something held him back—another voice in Judas that said: "If you do, you will look like Miriam!" No, his love for the Master, though more extreme than that of any of the other disciples, was a higher form of love and must therefore remain secret in its dignity rather than degrade itself in emotional and sentimental acts.

Nevertheless, this was such a powerful moment between them—surely the others sensed something.

Now Yeshua began to speak: "I know you all. I know you, whom I have chosen. The scripture must be fulfilled, the one that says:

> Even my dear friend in whom I trusted, who ate of my bread,
> has lifted his heel against me.*

"I tell you now, before it all happens,so that when it does happen, you will believe that I AM."

Yeshua smiled at Judas, who was trembling.

"What a wretched man I am!" Judas thought. "Better never to have been born than have this task: to deliver to his enemies the one human being I love more than any other! But it must be done, so that he may reveal himself and the will of Adonai be done."

---

*Psalms 41:9.

# 19

## *The Last Supper*

As they ate, Yeshua took some bread, blessed it, and broke it, saying: "Take this and eat it, for it is my body."

Then, taking a cup of wine, he blessed it and held it up to them, saying: "Drink this, for this is my blood. It is the blood of the covenant, which shall be given for the many in remission of their sins. I tell you, I myself shall drink no more of the fruit of the vine until the day when I drink it anew with you in the Kingdom of my Father."

Andrew was astonished at these words. But Philip smiled, explaining to him: "For the sages of our tradition, bread and body symbolize action. What he is saying is: Do as I have done, act as I have acted, and you will see that I AM. Also, wine and blood symbolize both contemplation and our intimate life. By telling us to drink his blood, he means: Contemplate what I have contemplated, and share my intimacy with the Father so that you will become what I AM. This intimate life is also a gift (as in blood that is shed), and here we discover the true covenant with I AM, the One who gives all being. Then we will be aligned with our true axis as sons of YHWH. We will live no more in sin, missing the mark of our true being."

Andrew answered: "For us, there remains a mystery. The meaning of what Yeshua says and does is hidden and unfathomable. Yet for you this mystery is understandable. Which interpretation is right: yours or ours?"

Philip had no time to reply, for Yeshua had begun to speak.

"Have I not spoken clearly enough? One of you will deliver me."

They heard him well enough, but they were confused. Had he not just spoken of his body and his blood as a gift to the many, like the gifts of his acts, his words, and his prayers? Did *deliver* not have a double meaning? Did it not mean "bring out" as well as "betray"? Perhaps only Judas fully understood the power of this double meaning. To betray him so that he reveals himself for himself, to all . . . But the other disciples were disturbed and confused, each wondering "Could it be me?"

Peter whispered to Yohanon, who was standing next to the Teacher, "Ask him who it is."

Leaning toward Yeshua, Yohanan whispered, "Who is it?"

"It is the one to whom I give the first bread, the first to receive communion with what the gift of my life means."

And he took a piece of bread, dipped it in the wine, and gave it to Judas. The latter was trembling again, but as soon as he took the bread, he felt better and steadier. It was as if a power that would enable him to accomplish the impossible had entered him. He thought of Shatan, that other son of God mentioned in the Book of Job, the one whom YHWH sent to test human beings to reveal what is in their hearts.

Then Yeshua said to Judas: "What you must do, do it quickly."

No one else understood what he meant. Because Judas was the treasurer, some supposed that Yeshua was referring to purchases that had not yet been made—money for the poor, perhaps.

Judas left the room. The bread lingered in his mouth, radiant, as if it had been soaked in light rather than wine.

Night had come.

Yeshua then said: "Now the Son of Man will reveal his glory. YHWH will be present in him and manifest his greatness."

Then they all began to chant together, singing from the Psalms. Finally, they left for the Mount of Olives.

Yeshua spoke to them again, saying: "All of you will succumb because of me, this very night. It has been written that I shall strike the shepherd and the sheep will be dispersed. But after my resurrection, I will precede you into Galilee."

Now Peter spoke: "Even if everyone succumbs and betrays you, I will never do so!"

Yeshua answered him: "This very night, before the cock crows, you will renounce me three times."

Peter objected strongly: "I will never renounce you, even if I must die with you!"

The other disciples supported him, and took the same vow.

Meanwhile, Judas was on his way to see the high priests to inform them where Yeshua could be found in the early hours of the morning. Let them do what they would! Things were turning out very different from what he had thought, dreamed, and hoped—but he was certain that the unfathomable destiny of Yeshua was in motion.

The priests gave him thirty pieces of silver as reward for this information. Thirty coins—a trivial sum compared to the price of the oil Miriam had lavished on the feet of the Teacher. Again, Judas thought of using the money to buy arms, but he remembered how adamantly Yeshua had refused to be involved in armed struggle. Surely, it was through his inner power and magic that he would drive out the Roman soldiers.

He almost told the priests to keep their money. His heart wanted to say: "Do you think you can buy the Messiah or buy me for delivering him? How could a trivial sum of money ever console me for such a crime? Only his victory can console me!"

# 20

# *The Arrest*

For Judas, the most difficult task of all was now before him. Denouncing Yeshua to the high priests had been easy because he had nothing but contempt for such men. But to deliver him directly to the Romans—that was a different matter. In having Judas do this, Yeshua was asking the disciple to go against what had been his lifelong ideal: to drive these occupiers out of the Holy Land, to liberate the poor and innocent who groaned under the Roman yoke, with all its violence and injustices. Now, because of his love for the Messiah, he must consort with the enemy of Israel! He would have need of great faith and confidence in the strategy Yeshua had inspired in him in order to tarnish this ideal.

He murmured a prayer so that those around him could not hear: "Adonai, Elohim, help me! Yeshua, do not abandon me!"

Then he took his place at the head of the troop of centurions and other armed men who had been paid by the high priests.

They arrived upstream from the rapids of the Cedron, where there was a garden. Yeshua often came there with his disciples. Judas had told the soldiers that he would kiss the man they were to arrest—but even at this point, Judas could not really imagine Yeshua's arrest actually occurring. Would not the Messiah choose this moment to reveal himself, sending forth a fire that would consume the soldiers?

He approached Yeshua confidently and gave him the kiss of disciple to Master. "Rejoice, Rabbi!" Judas said. Yeshua answered, simply: "My friend."

The disciples awoke as if from a troubled sleep and were surprised to see Yeshua and Judas surrounded by armed men. At first they thought Judas had brought his Zealot friends for protection, but when they recognized the armor of the Roman centurions, they became very afraid.

Yeshua advanced calmly toward the group of Roman soldiers. "Whom do you seek?" he asked.

"Yeshua of Nazareth."

"I am he."

When he spoke these words, the soldiers were strangely startled, stumbling backward, and several even fell down. Judas was elated: Finally, it was beginning! Even the Romans could be affected by the divinity of this Name. Its power had forced them back—and this was only the start!

But Judas's joy was short-lived.

Again, Yeshua asked them: "Whom do you seek?"

"Yeshua of Nazareth!"

"I have told you: I AM. If it is I whom you seek, then let the others go."

Then Peter, who had drawn his short sword, struck Malchus, the servant of the high priest, cutting off his right ear.

But Yeshua remonstrated with Peter: "Put away your sword! He who lives by the sword shall die by the sword."

Then he looked at Judas, who also stumbled backward at his glance.

"If I wished, I could oppose a troop of angels to your troop of soldiers. But the cup that the Father has given me—must I not drink it?"

And he surrendered himself to the chief of the Roman legion.

Judas was devastated. Was this all the resistance the Messiah would offer—a brief demonstration of his power, and then surrender? Also, his refusal of Peter's sword was clearly a refusal of Judas's dagger as well. Once more, Judas felt humiliated and betrayed.

What was Yeshua trying to accomplish? If he had been simply a coward, why would he have refused the help of the sword? "The Book and the sword": Was that not the motto of true upholders of the faith? Did Yeshua not know that the Book without the sword was powerless, just as the sword without the Book was blind? Were not the holy scriptures written in order to guide the sword, directing it against evil? Killing infidels had never counted as murder, but rather as an act of purification. To balk at this was like balking at a physician's extermination of noxious vermin. Did not real crime consist of allowing the just to be killed?

Now Peter began to shout, pointing at Judas: "He is the one who delivered him!"

Judas was stunned. He had only been obeying his Master, even to the point of going against his own intimate convictions, his very honor—and now he was being accused of treason! Why was he to blame for Yeshua's strange behavior, for the Master's refusal to behave as the powerful man they saw in him? Why blame him for Yeshua's capitulation before the battle had even begun?

"Peter!" Judas shouted back. "It was not I who told you to put away your sword! My dagger was ready to join you in defending him—and we have armed allies hiding in the forest around here, waiting for my sign to attack. But you saw it yourself—he gave himself up to his persecutors!"

Now Yohanan, Philip, Jacob, and Peter all began to shout excitedly. "Quick, Judas! Call your men! We must go rescue him!"

"How do you rescue a man who refuses to be rescued?" Judas answered harshly. "You know as well as I do how strong his will is when he has made a decision. We cannot go against it. We have been fooling ourselves! This man does not stand for the life or freedom of his people! He is filled with a morbid desire for suffering. He seeks death. Well, now he is on his way to finding what he wants. As for me, I want nothing more to do with him."

"Judas!" Miriam cried. "It is now that you are betraying him! It is now that you forsake all your faith in him!"

Judas gave way to a violent impulse and shoved her roughly so that she crumbled and fell upon the dusty ground. But he felt as if he himself were about to crumble and fall, although he was still standing straight and boiling with rage and despair. Little by little, he began to see what he had done. It was if he were emerging from a dream that had lasted for years.

His dream had been of a Messiah, a Messenger sent to deliver Israel and, through Israel, all of humanity. He had appointed Yeshua as the Messiah of his dreams . . . but now that his dream was shattered for good, he was left with only a pathetic, weak Roman prisoner named Yeshua, one no more courageous or powerful than an average man, one who had capitulated shamefully before the forces of injustice. Faced with the Romans, he would not even resort to the sword of his words or the fire of his regard to defend himself! Yeshua was like a dog who could no longer even bark, blinder than the blind ones whom he had amused himself by healing—and was all that not a mere bag of tricks to distract everyone from the essential?

"Miriam, you are right. I no longer believe in him. I wonder if I ever did. Perhaps I only dreamed it all. . . . In this dream, I believed in the justice of God, in the Law that holds us in the dignity, integrity, and nobility of a Chosen People. Yes, I believed with all my soul—or did I only dream it?—in the Word that promises us that the poor are not forgotten and that a Messiah will come as our savior. . . . Now that I no longer believe in my Messiah, my King, this son of David . . . will I also begin to doubt the Law, the Torah itself? Will I even doubt YHWH, God of gods, the Creator of heaven and earth?"

Judas grunted and collapsed to the ground. He then began crawling as an animal, grabbing handfuls of grass and eating them and even eating handfuls of earth. "The earth! There is no other reality! All is made of dust and returns to dust. Why bother to stand? The serpent was right! It is closest to reality, caressing the earth with every inch of its skin, with all its scales! The earth is the single reality. We dreamed that we had a soul, but that soul is only a dream of the earth, the bud of an ephemeral flower carried away by a mudslide . . ."

The other disciples were alarmed and horrified. "Judas, you're delirious and raving!" they cried.

"You'll see if I'm delirious," he sneered. "Go follow your master now! See for yourselves what sort of man he is. He'll let himself be crucified like a common thief! . . . O Yeshua! Why did you mislead us like this? Maybe the Pharisees were right when they said you were possessed by a demon . . . a clever demon, a less sad demon than the one haunting me right now, pulling me into the abyss of doubt and blasphemy. . . . But to each the demon he deserves . . . to each his own trial to be endured so that he may know himself."

Judas leapt up and hurried away, heading for the Temple. When he arrived in the chamber where the high priests were seated, he threw at them the thirty pieces of silver and cried: "I have delivered an innocent man to you. This Yeshua is only a pathetic madman—neither the Messiah you feared nor the one for whom I hoped. He deceived us with his great, beautiful eyes and his honeyed words. Let him go—he's harmless to you and to the Romans. No men or even children will follow him any more—the only thing he's good for now is seducing lost women."

The high priests paid little attention to this outburst, but one of them took the pieces of silver, saying: "We cannot return this money to the treasury, for it is blood money." After conferring with each other, they decided to use the money to buy the potter's field as a burial ground for foreigners. To Judas, they replied: "What is done is done. Now we must let the men of the Law fulfill their duty."

"Law? What Law?" Judas muttered, walking away. "There is no Law. There is no God. The only Law is that of the strong against the weak. Today, it's the Romans; tomorrow it will be someone else."

Outside, Judas fell once more upon the ground, gathering handfuls of mud and smearing it in his hair. "Holy dirt! Deliver me from my dreams of justice! Heal me from those pathetic, idiotic beliefs that keep people staring dizzily at an empty sky, imagining someone who lives there other than vultures, clouds, and bloodsucking insects . . . and you, poor old sun, every day you seem a little paler, eaten away by the night . . ."

He staggered out of the gates of Jerusalem.

# 21

## *The Praetorium*

Judas was lying inert on the ground, not far from the potter's field.* Jacob shook him awake.

Judas stood up and spoke angrily: "Even during the night, he haunts me! What potion can I drink to stop these dreams? In one of them, I saw Yeshua, shining and standing with Moshe and Eliahu . . ."

"But that is exactly what we saw on Mount Tabor!" exclaimed Jacob.

"Yes, but all that proves is that you have the same ridiculous dreams! Have you still not understood? This man who convinced you that he came to fulfill the Law and the prophets is an impostor!"

"If so," Jacob replied, "then this imposter loves us as no man has ever loved. This morning, Peter followed him all the way to the house of Caiaphas, the high priest. But as he stood outside near the door, a maid recognized him, saying: 'Aren't you one of the disciples of this man?' Peter answered, 'No, I am not.' Some of the other servants and guards had built a fire, and were warming themselves.

*Later, this would be called Hakeldaima, "land of blood."

They, too, asked Peter: 'You, with the Galilean accent—aren't you one of his disciples?' Again, he answered, 'No, I am not.' Then one of the personal servants of the high priest, a relative of the man whose ear Peter cut off, came out. Looking at Peter suspiciously, he said: 'Weren't you among the disciples of that man in the garden tonight?' Then Peter stood up and swore, 'No! I tell you, I am not his disciple, and I do not know this man!' Then the cock crowed, and Peter began to weep bitter tears, for he remembered what the Teacher had said: 'You will deny me three times before the cock crows.'"

"You see?" Judas replied. "Everything was predetermined! We are nothing but his puppets; he puts us in situations where we will have to deny him, yet it is he who has denied us—for he is a manipulator and a traitor!"

"There was one thing that wasn't predetermined," Jacob replied calmly. "When Yeshua left the house of the high priest, it happened that Peter was standing in his way. I swear to you, Judas, there was not the slightest hint of accusation or judgment in his eyes. His look was like that of a child—a child whom each of us has either betrayed, tortured, abandoned, or scorned. Peter cried again upon seeing him, but this time his tears were not bitter. You see, Judas, the fault may sometimes be predetermined—but never the forgiveness."

"Who can truly forgive but YHWH himself?" Judas answered.

"That's exactly the point. If Yeshua was able to forgive Peter, it was because YHWH was with him. Is not the Almighty that Yeshua bears witness to the Almighty of forgiveness, love, and compassion?"

"Shut up with your nonsense!" Judas cried. "What can this Almighty of love do against my refusal? I say no to this love! Can this Almighty force me to love or to believe in him? So where is he now, your rabbi with the Almighty in him—down on his knees before a Roman soldier? Don't you see what Yeshua's game is? He manipulates us into betraying him so he can forgive us, and then he weakens us by showing what great forgiveness and love he is capable of giving. I've had enough of him! He has abused us, and I no longer believe in him at all. If he came here right now with dewy eyes and his hand over his heart, ready to forgive me, I'd spit in his face! I don't want forgiveness, Jacob! Forgiveness for what? For believing in him? For believing in YHWH? How can anyone pardon me when I cannot pardon myself for my stupidity, my idiotic faith and submission to a God who doesn't exist? How can I forgive myself for confusing my own dreams of purity with reality? There has never been anything but me, the earth, and the sun—and even the sun has to die every night. What can I do to forget this stupid dream, forget myself . . . except to go hang myself?"

"That is forbidden by the Law of our God," Jacob replied.

"This God is a dream, and so is his Law. Now that I've stopped dreaming, what's to stop me from killing others—or myself?"

"Never forget that Yeshua loves you and that he chose you—for him, you are unique."

"Yes, that's part of the dream, just like the rest of it. It's a dream I want to forget, and only death can make me forget it. Only death can prevent me from dreaming . . ."

"Judas, it is not only Yeshua who loves you; it is also YHWH himself, for he created you."

"Yes, just as he created vipers, vultures, and all these other animals who devour other creatures before being devoured themselves."

"YHWH means the One Who Is, the One who causes you and the whole universe to be. You must believe this, Judas." Jacob was now pleading: "God is love. Yeshua has taught us this, and now he is living this truth through his very flesh and his endless patience . . ."

"God is love!" Judas sneered. "I'd like to see some evidence of that!"

"Come, then, and you will see," Jacob answered, taking him by the hand.

And they went toward the praetorium, where Yeshua was appearing before Pontius Pilate.

It was morning and a crowd had gathered. Some pious Jews were standing away from the porch, not wanting to touch the praetorium steps to avoid pollution. Pilate himself came forward, and spoke to them:

"What charges do you bring against this man?"

"If he was not a criminal, we would not have brought him to you."

"Then take him and judge him according to your own Law."

"We are not allowed to apply the death penalty."

Then Pilate turned back and said to Yeshua: "Are you the king of the Jews?"

"Are you asking this for yourself or because others have said it of me?" Yeshua answered.

"Am I a Jew, to interest myself in this?" Pilate said. "Your people and your high priests have delivered you to me. What have you done?"

"My Kingdom is not of this world. If my Kingdom were of this world, my friends would have engaged in battle." As he said this, he looked far into the crowd, as if searching for Judas.

"How dare he say that, the wretch!" Judas exclaimed to Jacob. "Not only has he abandoned us, but now he stands before the enemy, denying us as warriors as well! He only pretended to be one of us, but he is not on our side. Is this what you call love, Jacob?" But Jacob ignored him, for he was listening intently to Yeshua.

Pilate then said: "So—then you *are* a king?"

"It is you who say it: I AM King. I came into this world and was born only to bear witness to the truth. Whoever is of the truth hears my voice."

"What is Truth?"*

Yeshua was silent.

Judas was disgusted at this. "You see? He can't answer, this king of ours! He doesn't even know what truth is—or else he knows that it doesn't really exist. This golden tongue is paralyzed when the real questions are asked! How can he say what truth is when he is full of lies?"

"Look at him," Jacob answered calmly. "Look how he stands face-to-face with Pilate, before the crowd. They treat him as a criminal and he stands with the dignity of a king. He has nothing to say, for he is what he is. He does not define what truth is, for he *is* the truth. Yeshua has not been teaching us about a truth we can possess, but instead offering us the example of a truth we can *be,* even in the face of adversity, injustice, and the arrogance of power. What Yeshua has given us cannot be made by us into a possession of knowledge or power. What he offers us is to *be* more, to grow in consciousness and in love. The Kingdom of which he speaks is the world of true human beings."

These words of Jacob's suddenly reminded Judas of Yeshua's own words in the desert. Yes, the message was consistent, he had to admit—but Judas's opinion had not changed. It was sheer nonsense. It appealed only to people with full bellies and empty brains. It would never mean anything to those who were starving not only for food, but also for justice.

"Look at him, Judas, how bravely he stands!"

"For how long? Soon you will see him groaning on a cross and lying in a tomb. And he will never stand again."

"What do you know?" Jacob replied. "The other day, you were saying just the opposite."

---

*John 18:38.

"I've had enough of all this," Judas replied, wearily.

During this time, Pilate had come back to address the crowd.

"I find no grounds for condemning this man. It is the custom for me to release a prisoner for your holy day of Passover. Shall I release the king of the Jews?"

"No!" the crowed roared. "Not him! Release Barabbas instead!" And everyone began to chant in unison: "Barabbas! Barabbas!"

Both Jacob and Judas were mute in the face of this mass hysteria all around them. Judas felt nauseated again. He had recognized some in the crowd who, only a short time before, had been shouting for Yeshua, the Messiah. "Is not each of us a mere thread," he thought, "woven into the net of this imbecilic crowd of humanity? One day it shouts 'Long live the King!' The next day it shouts 'Death to the King!'"

He knew Barabbas well. A real bandit, that one, who never joined with the Zealots, for his only cause was his own profit. Yet the crowd had made the right choice after all, Judas reflected. Brigands are less dangerous than liars who make us dream . . . at least they don't pretend to be someone else, and we know what to expect of them and are prepared to defend ourselves with violence against them.

Pilate then led Yeshua off to be whipped. The soldiers had woven a crown of thorns and placed it on Yeshua's head, dressing him in a mantle of royal purple. First they made mock obeisance before him, saying: "Hail, king of the Jews!" Then they began to lash him.

Judas observed the strange serenity of Yeshua as the blows fell upon him. Suddenly he thought of those children murdered by Herod, supposedly because the Messiah had just been born in Bethlehem. He had a vision of soldiers tearing babies away from their mothers' breasts and smashing them against walls running with blood. Were these the sort of horrors that Yeshua had come to exorcise or expiate? Was there no other way for him to bring peace and salvation than to take upon himself the guilt for all the sins of humanity?

Rather than denying or fleeing guilt as many sages had, he appropriated it upon himself. Perhaps he thought that whatever is not appropriated is not redeemed. Did he also assume guilt for those natural injustices for which human beings can find no explanation? If so, was he not taking on the role of God himself, the One, the maker of all that is?

No! Judas shook himself in an effort to banish this train of thought. No, he repeated to himself, I am not guilty for what my parents have done, nor for the actions of the Herods they served. I am not guilty for Herod's murder of innocents. I do not want peace at the price of assuming such guilt! I do not want to be saved by suffering. . . . And yet, how am I to escape the torment of my dreams, my nightmares? How can I ever find peace in a world ruled by violence and crime? If I kill myself to escape guilt and suffering, is that not just another crime? And what about the Law that forbids such a cowardly escape? Does Yeshua know any more about it than I? Does he assume the guilt of the world in order to transcend it? But I see no transcendence. . . . I see only the scream of one more innocent under the blows, adding itself to the screams of all the other innocents smashed against walls. I see nothing more, nothing but screams under an indifferent sky.

# 22

# *Behold, the Man*

After having Yeshua whipped, Pilate had him brought out in front of the crowd, and said: "You see, I bring him out before you so that you know that I find no grounds to condemn him."

Yeshua still wore the crown of thorns and the purple cloak the soldiers had placed upon him.

"Behold, the man!"*

When they beheld him, the high priests and the guards shouted: "Crucify him! Crucify him!"

Pilate answered them: "Crucify him yourselves, for I can find no grounds for condemning him."

"We have a Law, and it says he must die, for he claims to be the Son of God."

Pilate turned back to his prisoner and asked him: "Who are you?"

Yeshua was silent.

Why is he behaving so mysteriously? Judas wondered to himself. Everyone knows who this man is: He comes from Nazareth and has

*John 19:5.

parents, sisters, brothers. He's the son of a Galilean carpenter, not the Son of YHWH!

Pilate said: "You do not answer. Do you realize I have the power to release you or crucify you?"

Yeshua answered: "You have no power except that given to you from above."*

"Incredible!" Judas exclaimed. "He is actually standing up to Pilate—but with only words. Why does he not use the power he claims to have? He knows the Law: an eye for an eye, a tooth for a tooth. If he was really a man of power, a man of God, he would pay back the Romans for every lash of their whip and destroy countless hordes of soldiers and citizens to pay for all our men, women, and children they have destroyed—that would be real justice."

"That is exactly what he refuses to do—" replied Jacob, "—to reply to violence with violence. Has he not taught us to turn the other cheek? He is greater than his anger, and his replies are natural and just, for he is speaking to the conscience of his enemies."

"Jacob, you are dreaming again! What conscience? The conscience of those Romans? Israel's enemies have never had a conscience. Turning the other cheek is just inviting the enemy to massacre us."

"But if faced with the choice—to cause suffering or to suffer—which is nobler? Look at Pilate—even he is affected by Yeshua's presence."

"*You* look—and watch what happens next," Judas muttered.

Pilate clearly wanted to release Yeshua, but the crowd began to shout angrily: "If you release him, you are no servant of Caesar! Anyone who claims to be king is the enemy of Caesar!"

Hearing these words, Pilate had Yeshua led to Gabbatha, or the Pavement, where he then sat in judgment at the tribunal.

---

*John 19:11.

It was around the sixth hour and during the Passover preparation. Pilate addressed the crowd once more: "Behold, your king!"

"Death to him! Death to him! Crucify him!" they roared.

"You would have me crucify your king?" Pilate asked.

"We have no king but Caesar!" they shouted.

Then Pilate delivered Yeshua to them to be crucified.

"There you have it, the end of the story," Judas sneered. "Behold, the man! A beautiful ideal, a deluded dream, a futile passion! You say he loved? He certainly believed he loved us, all of us—Miriam, Peter, Yohanan, the crippled, the possessed—yes, he loved the whole world, but for what? For this?"

"Love is its own reward," Jacob answered.

"No, our only reward is death—for the just and the unjust alike! Instead of defending himself, escaping, or leading an ordinary life, Yeshua had to do things on a grand scale, with a pride to match his eloquent words. And, faithful to the logic of his supreme pride, he allows himself to be crucified."

"They are not taking his life," Jacob replied. "He is giving it."

"Quite right—death will take anything you give it—and take it whether you give it or not!"

But now Judas felt a sudden weakness. Seeing Yeshua led like a common criminal toward the hill of Golgotha, he felt a pain in his heart such as he had never known before. It was perhaps the first time in his life (except for his first meeting with Yeshua) that he really felt his heart and knew that he had one. But if he allowed that feeling too much room, the pain would become unbearable, the sadness and grief would be incurable.

He continued: "And what is the fate of a person afflicted with this disease called Yeshua—never to die? Who can say? But this much is certain: They will never be cured!" Judas was sure of only one thing: He did not want to be contaminated by this disease! He hardened himself inwardly and immediately found that he returned to his normal self—his implacable, despairing lucidity was still intact.

"Now leave me, Jacob—I want to be alone and I'm not following you the rest of the way to see him hang on the cross. I've seen enough crucifixions in my time—so many Zealot friends, men of faith and justice . . . for the Romans, this is all routine. Our blood oils the wheels of their empire! I've seen the shedding of enough innocent blood, and so has our land. I've given up on heaven, and now even the earth seems shaky beneath my feet, like quicksand, or sinister mud drenched with blood, rotting flesh, and bones . . . like a mother who grinds up her children and eats them. She brought us into the world, with all our crazy ideals, only for us to serve as fertilizer for her when we get tired of playing the game. I'm tired, Jacob, and I want to die—just as Yeshua does, no doubt. I've had enough of this bloody farce. I was born the same day he was, the day when Herod massacred all those innocent children, and now I shall die on the same day he dies, at the same time: yet another day when innocents are murdered. For this is how things will continue, until the end of the world."

## 23

# *Death*

Indeed, Judas had seen many men hanging on crosses in his time. The Romans often displayed them prominently so they would be visible to all as people entered a village, and of course along the road leading from Jerusalem to Jericho. At this point, death was his only certainty, and he was not afraid of it. Why fear the obvious? Death and life were the same illusion, his reason told him. Yet something in him remained unsatisfied. Perhaps there was something beyond reason . . . his heart, that burning pain he had felt upon seeing Yeshua led to be crucified?

But looking into his heart, into his deepest feelings, was sheer hell to him now. "This hell can exist only because God is love," he thought. "It is because of my heart that I can still live in hell. I would have to annihilate love, tear out my heart, to stop this suffering. Yet that would be even worse than the suffering."

Once again, his thoughts turned to Job as to an old friend. It was the first scripture that had ever moved him when he was a child, and later, during his studies. Job had lost everything—his home, his property, his wealth, then his children, his family, his friends, and his health. He found himself alone on a heap of dung, alone with God—a God he had imagined himself so he would not feel so alone! A God he had thought to be just and good—but it was in vain that he asked justice from this God. Now, it was time to let this imaginary God of justice and goodness disappear. Then, nothing would remain. He would be alone—so alone! Job did not have the courage to bear this, did not have the courage to kill himself. But he, Judas, did have the courage . . .

What use is it to insult God if you don't have the courage to destroy his so-called masterpiece of Creation, this wondrous creature of violence and hypocrisy supposedly made in his image?

Job had lost all that he cherished, including his greatest love of all: his love for a God of goodness who gave meaning to Job's own life of good works, faith, and kindness. How could he remain standing after such a loss?

At this, Judas fell once more to the ground, lying on his belly, clawing at the earth, wailing, and writhing like a serpent. He did not notice the clouds covering the sky and becoming ominously darker by the minute.

"Job, my friend! Job! Why didn't you kill yourself? Everyone would have understood—no one would have denied you an honorable burial. But perhaps . . . perhaps the Book contains a lie . . . perhaps someone invented that ridiculous end to your story, Job, bringing in an impressive God with the story of Leviathan and all those other hallucinations in order to intimidate anyone who might dare to argue with God . . . The Book claims you said: 'Until now I had only heard of You, but now my eyes have seen You . . .'* But if your eyes really saw him, Job, then you would have to die yourself . . . So that's how all your wealth, your friends, your wife, your sons and daughters were returned to you when you called them each by name. Perhaps you have to be dead to

*Job 42:5.

retrieve what you have lost—not like a debt, but like a gift. . . . The Teacher used to say: 'You must die in order to be reborn.' But what does that mean? I'm like you, Job, I'm raving, delirious, talking too much . . . but there may be more wisdom in this delirium than in those words of righteous wisdom and justice with which I used to think I could guide others. . . . When did you see God, Job? Just before you died? At the moment of death? Or was it afterward? 'My eyes have seen You, and I cover myself with dust and ashes'*—that's what you said, but I still see nothing, Job. No heaven, no earth, only myself. . . . What did your eyes see? What have my eyes seen?"

Now his entire body suddenly began to tremble, and he lifted his garment over his eyes, as if to veil himself: "My eyes have seen *you,* Yeshua! I should have torn them out, but now it's too late. . . . YHWH: None has ever seen him and lived . . . but you, Yeshua, I have seen . . . and even if you betrayed me, I never saw anything so good and so beautiful as you, even if you were only a dream. The only meaning in all my life was when you looked at me in this dream . . ."

And then Judas's body was wracked with a great cry, which came from his very depths:

*"Eli, Eli, lama sabakhtani?*
Yeshua, Yeshua, why have you abandoned me?
YHWH, why have you abandoned me?"

Judas was weeping. At the same time, a great storm was raging. His entire body seemed to have melted into a mixture of water, blood, and earth, like the red clay with which he was covered, the *adamah* of which the Book says YHWH made humanity.

---

*Job 42:6.

# 24

## *Resurrection*

At the very moment that Judas cried out, there was an earthquake. The storm filled the sky with thunder, lightning, and then rain.

How long did he lie there, motionless in the mud, his arms stretched out in the form of a cross? A day, at least—two, perhaps three? A woman passed by and saw him awaken. It was as if he had awakened from a nightmare. Though damaged by the heavy storm, the land around him seemed like a beautiful garden.

"I am dead. Or am I alive? In any case, I AM."

As he spoke these words, Yeshua's presence returned to him—in his heart, not his memory—and he was filled with a strange feeling.

"Before Abraham was, I AM."

What joy! Previously, these words of Yeshua's had always been as incomprehensible as a foreign language. Now, at last, he understood. Tears of joy washed away the dregs of memory of the last few days.

"They killed him, but he is alive!" Judas thought. Now, he no longer doubted that this was a dream or an illusion.

"He killed me, and I AM alive! He killed my Messiah, my God, everything I held most precious . . . and I AM alive! He dragged me through the mud and in the mud gave me a kiss, a breath . . . and I AM alive! He came into my tomb, took the rope from around my neck, and closed up the wound in my belly. He respected my despair, my fascination with nothingness. When I spat my hatred of love in his face, he made a balm of it, for suffering is cured only by suffering; death is conquered only through death.

"It is not suffering, however, that saves and heals; it is the consciousness in which it is experienced. It is not the cross we bear that saves and heals us; it is the love with which we bear it. It is not death that saves and heals; it is the fearlessness and trust in which we enter it.

"Look at my neck, my strangled throat, my fingernails . . . yes, that is Judas: I died, and I AM alive. I descended into hell. Falling in the abyss, I experienced not just vertigo, but also that slow decay of bones, flesh, and thoughts. . . . I experienced that suffocation, that burning of rejected love, that wounded child's look, like a heartbreaking little God, a gentle flame on which we slam the door . . . but the patience of that flame, like that of love, will finally open all doors, and the patience of water, like that of tears, will finally dissolve the thickest walls.

"I descended into hell and saw there the beings in despair. I saw those who have committed horrendous crimes—and the worst crime of all is to have no regret for our crimes. I saw my brothers and sisters, the suicides. . . . Now, of course, we know how useless suicide is . . . there is no escape in death. The important thing is to discover the I AM, whether it wears the face of Yeshua or of another messiah,* whether it appears as the ocean or as a tree with fathomless roots, whether it moves as the wings of a bird, or opens as the eyelashes of the One who looks into our eyes.

---

*The only false messiah is one who claims to be the only messiah.

"Stupidity, arrogance, lies, violence, injustice, hatred, and death will never have the last word, for these are only half of the real, they are only half of our path. Yet intelligence, humility, truthfulness, kindness, justice, love, and life will also never have the last word. They, too, are but half of the real, half of our path.

"Judas and Yeshua: We are the two halves of a human being. Only when we are brought together can there be a fully human being. Judas and Yeshua: We are the two paths that surely reveal a greater divinity of God.

"It is neither good nor evil that will have the last word. They are the two halves that compose a human being. . . . And beyond good and evil, beyond these two halves, another road begins."

# Appendix A

## *Reflections on an Enigma*

*To Olivier Clément,*
*who reminded me that among the members of my family (that of Orthodox Christianity) is Dostoyevsky*

### *Who Is Judas?*

Why must we always treat history and myth as if they are adversaries? Historical figures have often become myths, and sometimes a myth becomes so powerful that the historical figure recedes into the background.

When we consider the mythic Don Juan, how much are we really interested in the "real" Don Juan? Today, historians say that the historical Don Juan probably existed and lived near Seville . . . as did Carmen. In the same way, they say that Judas probably existed: a Judaean, perhaps a Zealot, whose family may have been close to the Herods.

The myth of the traitor, that archetypal figure of the gospel drama, makes us forget that there was probably a real Judas among the twelve disciples chosen by Yeshua. Likewise, the archetypal Miriam of Magdala has been discussed as a figure constructed from several of the women close to Yeshua. Here, too, the archetype has carried the day, and it is as an archetype that she has continued to live through the centuries.

Some would even claim that Yeshua himself is a construction put together by his disciples after his death: that they made of him a resurrected Messiah, the archetype of a savior or liberator—not only of his people, but of all humanity as well.

Yet Yeshua, Miriam, and Judas also refer to archetypes who exist before they manifest in the world. Yeshua is the incarnation of the "archetype of Synthesis,"* or the "figure of the Good," in the flesh. Likewise, Judas would be the figure, or the *typos,* of Evil, and Miriam the archetype of the woman who sins and is forgiven or, again, that of the Beloved, or of Sophia, the spouse of Logos.

Why this difficulty in accepting the fact that historical figures can become mythic figures? Conversely, why do people deny that myths, or archetypes, have incarnated in historical figures? History and myth are inseparably linked, if only for the simple reason that history is always a story—a story that must be interpreted and told.

In the case of Judas, what are the foundations—historical or mythic—of his story? As with Yeshua, there is no hard "scientific" evidence of his existence in Galilee or Judaea.

Archaeological and historical studies of documents of the period do allow us to reconstitute a hypothetical story that could be his—for example, to sketch a background of what may have been his relation to the politics of the period, involving the Romans, the Herods, the Sadducees, and so forth. We could also imagine him as a member

*This expression comes from Maximus the Confessor. It means a synthesis between the finite and the infinite, between eternity and time, and between human and God.

of the Zealots, like other disciples of Yeshua's were said to be. That would imply a potent feeling of revolt and outrage in the face of the "pollution" of the Roman occupiers and of the local authorities who collaborated with them.

Knowledge of the society in which Yeshua and his disciples lived has been greatly advanced recently by historical discoveries as well as by the unearthing of many lost scriptures (among them a gospel of Judas), which had been saved from suppression and buried for unknown reasons. Knowledge of the personalities who appear in the gospels, however, is, on the contrary, becoming more and more uncertain (though we must not equate certainty and knowledge).

Indeed, the discovery of these ancient texts compels us to revise our ready-made images, handed down through many centuries of Christian civilization: Many are shown to be no more than late fabrications composed by the religious authorities of the time. After reading, for example, the Gospels of Thomas, Mary Magdalene, and Philip, our old images of Yeshua and Miriam, as well as our images of the first Christian communities, cannot remain the same.

For our present purposes, however, it is toward the canonical scriptures (meaning those judged useful for the foundation of the institutional churches), rather than toward the so-called apocryphal or gnostic scriptures, that we shall turn in reconstructing the personality of Judas.*

We can discern a certain number of variants in the narrative of these events, notably between the acts reported in the Gospel of John and those of the synoptic gospels. An example is the scene of the anointing before the Last Supper: Did it happen in the house of

---

*See appendix B for these canonical texts in a translation that strives to stay close to the Greek originals. [The English translation of appendix B stays as close as possible to the author's French translation of the Greek. *The Gospel of Judas* mentioned by the author, edited by Rodolphe Kasser, Marvin Meyer, and Gregor Wurst, was published for the first time in 2006 by the National Geographic Society. Much of the Coptic original is still missing, but the picture of Judas that emerges from this gospel is radically different from that in the canonical gospels. —*Trans.*]

Simon (the "leper"), as is said in the Gospels of Mark, Matthew, and Luke? Or was it in Lazarus's house at Bethany, as the Gospel of John claims?

The best proof that the canonical gospels do not claim to be historical reports is the death of Judas. In Matthew 27:5, Judas hangs himself. Yet in the Acts of the Apostles (Acts 1:16–18), nothing is said about Judas killing himself; instead the Acts tells that he fell headfirst and that his body subsequently burst open.

These two versions each refer to different passages of the Hebrew scriptures. The first refers to 2 Samuel 17:23, where Ahitophel presents Absalom, the rebel son of David, with a plan to kill his father; but the counsel is rejected in favor of that of Hushai. "When Ahitophel saw that his counsel was not followed, he saddled his donkey, went to his house in the city, put it in order, hanged himself, and died." For the Gospel of Matthew, it was fitting that Judas hang himself as did Ahitophel, a traitor to the messiah-king David.

The version in the Acts of the Apostles refers to the Book of Wisdom 4:19, which says that "YHWH shall cast them down, mute, and headfirst."

The apocryphal gospels have still other variations on the death of Judas. All these versions serve to remind us that we do not know how Judas really died. They invite us to imagine his death according to the archetypal image we have of Judas so as to find the archetypal resonance that seems most fitting. This, of course, should not be confused with a claim as to how things happened historically.

The purpose of gospel scripture is not to answer our questions so that we no longer have to think. On the contrary, it is to question our answers, our habits, and our customs,* and to renew our way of thinking.

---

*See *The Gospel of Mary Magdalene,* when Peter says, "Must we change our customs, and listen to this woman?"

## *Metaphysical Foundations*

The affirmation of *what is* leads to the affirmation of the *Being that is and that causes what is to be*. The negation of *what is* leads to the negation of the same *Being*.

Behind the affirmation or negation of *what is* lies an opposition between two realities, which we shall call Being and Nothingness. But these opposites have "reality" only inasmuch as they affirm or deny *what is*. In other words, they are psychological realities.

Being and Nothingness describe the human power of affirmation or denial of what is. But then the question arises: What is *what is*? Is it neither Being nor Nothingness? Some call it the Unknown, Openness, or Emptiness.

But among these realities that are what they are, there is a body with a face that looks at me and speaks to me. This thing (a face, a body) encounters me through its openings. I meet it and relate to it with this thing in me, which is also an opening with a face that is able to give and receive.

This reality, this body that has a face and that speaks to me, may be called a subject. From now on, it is no longer simply *what is*—it is also *who is,* someone who is there, *this* person, *this* subject: you, I, he, she, *someone*.

The affirmation of *who is* leads to the affirmation of the One Being Who Is and who causes beings to be. This, we may say, is the same reality known to scripture as God, YHWH, and so forth. The negation of the One Who Is, who causes beings to be, is also the negation of God, or atheism.

The One Who Is and the One Who Is Not—as before, both of these realities are real only inasmuch as they represent an affirmation or denial. They are psychological realities. They describe the power of affirmation or negation of human beings faced with the One Who Is (the Subject of all Being or Reality that is given through *what is* or *who is*).

This power of affirmation or surrender and this power of refusal will determine the possibility of a relation between *someone who is* and the One Who Is. Some would describe this as a relation with the divine (or the sacred); others would describe it as a relation with God (or the holy).

A. A neutral relation to *what is* causes us to experience it as object, nature, world.
B. A positive relation to *what is* causes us to experience it as life, living nature, a sacred world.
C. A negative relation to *what is* causes us to experience it as fate, as a vale of tears, as a being that must die, as thrown out into existence.

A. A neutral relation to *who is* causes us to experience it as the principle of *what is,* as the First Cause, or Origin, of the subject of *what is,* the Source of freedom.
B. A positive relation to *who is* causes us to experience it as Presence of truth, of beauty, of love and as Father-Mother-Creator-Lord-Friend of each and all who are. This positive relation with *who is* in all-that-is is sometimes called Paradise, beatitude, joy, Nirvana, ecstasy, inner peace, and so forth. The incarnation of this positive relation may be seen in episodes from the story of Yeshua.
C. A negative relation with *who is* causes us to experience it as absence, lack, meaninglessness, absurdity, random fate, and so forth. It is the destruction of all subject in *what is.* It is the power represented by death, demon, and evil. This negative relation with *who is* in all who are is sometimes known as hell, the abyss, despair, anguish, acedia, and so forth. The incarnation of this negative relation may be seen in episodes from the story of Judas.

In the canonical gospels, the dramatic opposition between Yeshua and Judas can be seen as symbolizing the opposition between Being and Nothingness—as we have said, corresponding to positive and negative relations with *what is* and with *who is*. The opposition is also between hell and Paradise, and between a beautiful, beneficent, true, good incarnation that is a source of joy and freedom and an ugly, malevolent, dishonest incarnation that is a source of lies, despair, and alienation.

This would be the type of opposition compatible with Manichaeism—the God of Good against the God of Evil, the God of Yeshua and of the Christian scriptures versus the evil Demiurge, the God of Judas, the unjust God of the Hebrew scriptures.

My narrative about Judas challenges this kind of simplistic reductionism. In the first place, the challenge is metaphysical: Only Being *is;* Nothingness, by definition, cannot be. Therefore, it can mean only a psychological negation of *what is*. To affirm that Being *is* is more than just an affirmation of *what is*.

The neutral apprehension of *what is* does not posit any ultimate or supreme being in its affirmative apprehension. Nevertheless, in this neutrality, *what is* becomes an unknown *that,* unnameable, beyond representation.

The apophatic* apprehension of *what is* is neither an affirmation nor a negation. It does not constitute a negative philosophy or theology. It only denies the claim of language to be able to say *what is*—and, even more so, language's claim to be able to say *who is*. It remains closer to silent worship than to any other form of prayer or discourse.

In the gospel drama, it is clear that Yeshua incarnates a positive, affirmative relation to the Being Who Is, whom he calls "my Father and our Father." From the beginning to the end of his story (both in

*[*Apophasis* is an ancient theological tradition that considers God to be so ineffable that we can legitimately talk about only what God is *not*. —*Trans.*]

the gospels and in this narrative) he remains true to this affirmation in spite of his cry: "My God, why have you forsaken me?"—for his agony (from the Greek *agon,* meaning "struggle"—in this case, inner struggle) is evidence of a human flaw in his power of affirmation. Yet this only intensifies the humanity of his incarnation and reminds us that there is no faith without flaw and weakness; on the contrary, these serve as faith's activation and test. In the Book of Job, Satan is clearly a positive power, a son of God; yet he is also a negative power whose function is to test faith, to put it on trial.

The figure of Judas, however, seems less committed to evil than Yeshua is to good. He goes through phases of positive affirmation of *who is* and the One Who Is that manifest in his Teacher, and he also goes through phases of negative apprehension. No doubt this brings him closer to ordinary psychologies, with their contradictions and vacillations between opposites, which are very rarely integrated.

One might say that Judas first goes through a phase of positive affirmation when Yeshua heals the man who was blind from birth. The One Who Is is manifesting before him and seems to fulfill his hopes and expectations.

Then comes a phase of idealizing, when the One Who Is, manifest in Yeshua, becomes a kind of idol, an idealized dream Messiah. This hyperpositive affirmation can actually be seen as a negative one, because it loses all objectivity (i.e., any neutral apprehension of *what is* and *who is*) precisely through its hyperobjectification of its object of devotion.

But Yeshua does not allow Judas to remain in this state of excessive idealization. He shatters Judas's idol and his dream. Then the disciple, in his grievous disappointment with the reality of *who is,* feels betrayed and gives way to a negative apprehension of Yeshua. This logically culminates in a negative apprehension of YHWH himself and leads him to the final experience of Nothingness, which is known in many ancient traditions as the descent into hell.

This experience of Nothingness is not the end of Judas's adventure. Like hell, it has no ontological status of objective reality: Negation of Being is not a being.

As we have seen, by definition Nothingness can have no ontological reality, only a psychological one. But it does exist for me inasmuch as I subjectively refuse and deny Being, deny *what is* and *who is*. In a sense, this is a subjectivity that also refuses any relation between *what is* and *who is:* It denies any relation with the Other.

Nothingness does not exist and hell does not exist: This is what Judas discovers when he actually descends into hell. Here is what we might call the real gospel, or good news, of Judas:

Hell does not exist, for I have returned from it.
Hell is *myself*—
as long as I continue to deny *what is* and *who is*—
but this negation lasts only
as long as *myself* lasts.
Perhaps a long time,
but not an eternity!
When I have exhausted my capacity to deny,
to say no to *what is* and *who is;*
when I have exhausted
this ability to deny,
this ability that I have identified as *myself,*
then, in this transition from no to yes,
(from the *non serviam* to the *fiat*)*
it is no longer *myself* who lives,
but the I AM that lives in me . . .
I AM resurrected . . .

*[That is, from the *I will not submit* to the *let it be.* —*Trans.*]

## *Initiation*

Have not we all experienced what Judas experienced? Is not life an initiation? Is not our life the scene of our different passages* from one level of consciousness to another and one level of reality to another? Is not our life a continual series of deaths and resurrections? From birth on, we must die to the child we were in order to grow, we must die to the adolescent we were in order to become an adult. And a true adult must then die to certain self-images in order to become who we truly are, and then die again to that realization of *me* in order to discover the Self. We pass from this mortal being to Being that cannot die, in effect from this level of reality we call *I* (Judas, Simon, Yohanan) to have access to what I discover as the Being of I AM: the One Who Is forever (YHWH) inscribed in our being that passes.

I have previously published a study in French† of the stages in the evolution of consciousness, where I AM is realized through *eros* and *thanatos* and through *pleroma* and *kenosis*—in other words, through a thirst for fullness *(eros-pleroma)* and a fear of annihilation *(thanatos-kenosis)*.

The ending of each level of being (belonging to the known, or previously realized) is truly experienced as a death, which is the fundamental requirement for access to a higher level (still considered as unknown and unrealized). And access to this "new" reality is experienced as a "resurrection."

"Die before death": This is the ancient meaning of initiation. In this book I have attempted to present Judas as an initiate in this

*This is the original meaning of *pesach,* Passover. [It is also a striking example of the similarity of Semitic and Indo-European roots, supporting the now widely accepted thesis of a linguistic super-family called Afro-Asiatic. —*Trans.*]

†*Pleroma et kenosis: deux modes d'appréhension de l'Ouvert* [Pleroma and Kenosis: Two Modes of Apprehension of Openness] in *Tradition et modernité* (Paris: L'Originel, 1988).

sense—inasmuch as he, like Yeshua, goes to the very end of his humanity, which he exhausts, including physical death.

First he goes to the end of his hope and belief in the Messiah, and then he abandons them, recognizing them as illusory projections. Because his faith and hope also die along with his image of the Messiah, he goes past the end of all hope into a real fall into hell. It is there that he experiences his greatest passage, his Passover, in perfect resonance with that of Yeshua on the cross. At the moment when he loses his life and everything that gave it meaning (his God, his justice, his Messiah), he finds his true life.

At the moment when he loses his *me,* exhausted by despair, he finds the Self. Totally other than I, yet more I than *I,* he discovers the I AM, who he has been from all eternity, the I AM of which Yeshua spoke when he told his disciples: "There where I AM, I wish you to be also."

Because we do not really know how Judas died, we may assume that the gospel texts describe a death that is more symbolic than real. Without denying any of their symbolic truth, I have dared to say that Judas, like Yeshua, "died before death." In other words, he died to himself as a being separate from the I AM. In this sense, Yeshua was already resurrected before his physical death. Following the teaching of St. John, we might say that he lived already, in mortal form, the reality of eternal life (that dimension of eternity that lives in our ephemeral life).

It is not whether or not Judas really committed suicide that is important. In the abyss to which pain and despair had brought him, there is no more *I* to pose the question. "To be or not to be" is a valid (and no doubt tragic) question for this *I,* but it is no longer valid for one who has awakened to a reality beyond this *I,* beyond what it mistook for Being and Nothingness, entranced by its power of affirmation and negation. What abides is the I AM of the One Who Is, YHWH, the God anterior even to Being itself: the *agapē.*

I ask the reader to forgive me for what may seem like jargon. It is my attempt to indicate the enlightenment, or lightning flash, that frees us from our limits and returns us to life, consciousness, and infinite beatitude. In the language of the gospels, it is like walking out of the tomb.

## *Archetypal Resonances*

In ancient Christianity and before, notably among the *Therapeutae* of Alexandria mentioned by Philo, every biblical figure is considered an archetype, an image of a human destiny and evolution incarnated or manifested in a being who is usually historical. Thus Moses, Abraham, Noah, and Job are considered to have existed both historically and as archetypes, or structuring images, that can enter into resonance with our conscious and unconscious minds to clarify our becoming.

At certain moments in our own life story, we might therefore say "I am Abraham" or "I am Job." What Job or Abraham experienced can give meaning to what we are going through. Why cannot we say the same of Judas? Can we not enter into resonance with him by saying "I am Judas"?

At first glance this would seem far from easy. Entering into resonance with Yeshua brings us to the I AM, the uncreated light of our Being—yet Judas brings us into resonance with our shadow, with our power to refuse and negate the Being that offers itself, the I AM that is the love within us. If this Being of love is to be more than a dream, however, we must pass through the trials of despair, abandonment, and dereliction. No doubt we have all gone through this series of experiences: expectation, otherness, and disappointment. It is here that the path of Judas joins ours, at least for a time.

The path of Judas is that of a disappointed man, a Zealot (a word that signifies devotion as well as zeal), a man who had great expectations of Yeshua: not only that he was the righteous Teacher who would drive out the Roman occupiers, but also that he was the Messiah foretold by the sages and prophets of Israel. For Judas, as for the other disciples, Yeshua must be the human Godsend who would restore justice and peace in the Holy Land of their fathers.

As events developed, Yeshua no longer fit with these expectations. Judas felt betrayed: The Messiah refused to accept the power given him; nor would he give this power to Judas. Injustice, misery, and violence continued to oppress the country as before. The reign of God was not coming; there would be only more of the reign of Caesar.

Yeshua healed the sick, yet he did not heal all who asked him for healing. He resurrected Lazarus, but he did not behave as a man who has conquered death. He allowed himself to be vilified instead of calling down thunder and lightning upon his adversaries. Judas finally came to believe that Yeshua had capitulated, that he had "been had." His disappointment, like his expectation, was limitless.

A disappointed man is a dangerous man. Is not a betrayed man obliged to become a betrayer himself? Did not the Law of Moses say "an eye for an eye, a tooth for a tooth"? Yet the teaching of the gospels is that although this Law must be recognized within us, we must also recognize our ability to go beyond it.

This is how the figure of Judas can inspire us to reflect upon our own expectations: how it is that we expect of another that which we will not or dare not ask of ourselves. If our expectations are disappointed, it is only the expectations themselves that are to blame. But is it possible to live without expectations, to love without expectation—in other words, without illusion?

Undoubtedly, it is possible to live consciously in order to disengage ourselves a little more from our projections upon others and sometimes upon ourselves. But how can we avoid being trapped in disappointment? This trap is an important phase of the voyage of Judas, for he constantly maintains his disappointment by mulling it over and justifying it. This is, in a manner of speaking, what allows Satan to enter into him: the obstacle that shuts every door that might offer him a way out of his disappointment and toward the Other.

We might also say that he incarcerates himself in guilt for his treachery. Peter is also a traitor in his threefold denial of Yeshua. But unlike Judas, he believes that forgiveness is possible for him. When he meets the eyes of Yeshua, he weeps bitterly. It is through these tears that he is delivered from guilt and restored in his relationship with his Teacher. Now he can better exercise his role as a leader of the disciples, for his arrogance has been shattered: No longer can he pretend he is above betrayal—all it took was a challenge from a simple maid to make this pretension crumble.

It is interesting to note that Peter also shares another dubious privilege with Judas: that of being called a demon by the Teacher. When Yeshua announced that he was going to Jerusalem and would "suffer much at the hands of the high priests and scribes," Peter tried to detain him, saying "YHWH preserve you, that will not happen to you." Yeshua replied, "Get behind me, Satan; you are an obstacle to me, for your thoughts are not those of God, but of men."*

The person of Peter, however, does not become trapped in the negative consequences of his acts or words. He remains open to change, to possible repentance, which does not seem the case with Judas. The foundation of the drama described by the authors of the gospels is Judas's refusal of forgiveness, his refusal of the Other. This is also a refusal of any possible way out of his trap, which strangles him and leads him to "suicide."

He remains true to his concept of justice in that he pays for his acts. He does not believe in mercy and the possibility of grace, so he

---

*Matthew 16:21–23.

must hang himself. Here also we may see Judas in ourselves: In our fatal imprisonment in an ego for which there is no Other, no grace, no forgiveness, there may be times when we can see only "suicide" as a way out of the anguish and pain of this badly written farce called life.

Imprisonment in guilt, despair, or the absurdity of the human condition results when we style ourselves as *atheists* inasmuch as that term implies a closure to a possible Other, to a love greater than any misdeed: "Your own heart may condemn you, but God's heart is greater than yours."

The figure of Judas given to us by the churches is of little use. On the contrary, it adds even more guilt by presenting suicide as a terminal act that indefinitely imprisons us in a misdeed. Some would resort to the notion of eternal damnation—a metaphysical impossibility, given that the consequences of a finite act cannot be infinite. Judas thus becomes the archetype of the damned. His refusal or inability to be loved by love merits him a perpetual prison of torment: the image of an atheist whose tragic pride leads to the abyss.

But this picture of Judas is not true to the teaching of the gospels. Although his life is a dramatically tragic one, it still has this meaning: He did what he did "so that the scriptures may be fulfilled."

This notion of fulfillment is important. Without Judas, Yeshua would not have fulfilled his mission. He would have been more like Buddha or a prophet similar to previous prophets. Perhaps he would have lived to a ripe old age, continuing his sublime teaching of generosity and peace. But such a life would not have demonstrated or revealed in a human body and its deeds the invincible force of the humility of love in the face of absurdity, violence, and death.

The betrayal of Judas worked to reveal the I AM, YHWH, to which the life and teaching of Yeshua bear witness. This is why the gospel texts use the Greek word *paradosis* to refer to Judas's act (a word translated as "deliver" rather than "betray" and that also has associations of "transmission" and "tradition"). Hence Judas delivers the Light found within the deepest heart of darkness.

Following the methodology of the ancient Therapeutae and other exegetes, and considering the inner, universal meaning of this crucial moment of the gospels, we might say that in order for our program (i.e., our genetic code, which is also a kind of holy scripture) to be fulfilled, we must pass through the shadow. Instead of rejecting our shadow, we must integrate it. Otherwise, our other accomplishments will be in vain: With time, evil, repression, and negativity will eat away at us, poisoning our lives. The rejected shadow will break out, sooner or later, in the form of autonomous experiences that will have some power even over our realizations of the reality of *what is* and *who is.* Yet in truth, these autonomous manifestations originate in our own psychology—they are not independent of us.

Thus, evil itself in all its many forms (but especially in the forms of acedia, despair, and depression) actually contributes to our realization. As the saying goes: "For those who seek God, all things—even evil—conspire and work for the best." Even for those who no longer seek, even for those who despair and reject God, this truth applies. It is a question not of right or wrong, but of *what is.*

In spite of many people's assumptions about the Bible, its vision of God is actually nondualistic. God is not only the Creator of beauty and happiness:

> I create light and I create darkness, I create joy and I create grief, I am YHWH, who do all these things.*

It is not only along the paths of light, as incarnated by Yeshua, that YHWH leads us. It is also along paths of darkness, incarnated

*Isaiah 45:7.

by Judas. When Judas and Yeshua embrace, it is not only the meeting of darkness and light; it is a greater manifestation of God that is revealed and fulfilled.

Through this *coincidentia oppositorum,* in the outer story and in our inner story (grace versus absurdity), it is the great alchemy of the real that is fulfilled.

## *The Gospels of Judas*

The publicity surrounding the Gospel of Judas recently translated by Professor Kasser of the University of Geneva under the auspices of the Maecenas Foundation provides a good occasion to raise questions concerning the way gospels are redacted.

> In the first century of our era, many literate people were able to trace a few lines, but writing itself was a skilled profession: The scribe who exercised it had undergone a long training and in general was paid for his services. He possessed special materials: a tablet with an inkpot attached to it, a stylet with a dry point to mark the lines, and a scraper to erase them. He made his own inks, black or red, from smoke particles or from red clay that had been finely ground. From reeds or rushes he made pens, which he trimmed to obtain just the right thickness of line.*

In those days individuals wrote very slowly, and the paper (papyrus or parchment) was quite expensive. Hence, it is difficult to imagine the disciples writing down the words they had heard while they listened to the Teacher. Moreover, in the Jewish world of those days, as in societies of strong oral tradition that survive today, the direct transmission of the spoken word had more power than the written word.

---

*Michel Quesnel, *L'Histoire des Evangiles* (Paris: Cerf, 1987), 43.

The faith of those who would later be known as Christians was based not on books, but on the transmission of a breath *(pneuma)* and of a word *(logos)* that awakened in them the experience of a living Presence (unborn, uncreated), which they would later call the *anastasion,* the Resurrected. It was this living experience that served as the foundation of their questions and reflections about the Teacher who was the source of such a transmission and their later recollection of the memories of the last witnesses of the historical events necessary for the redaction of their *evangelion,* or good news.

This good news could be summarized in a few words: It is not absurd or in vain that we love, for Yeshua, who gave his life, murdered unjustly, is alive. He is resurrected. Stupidity, violence, hatred, and death do not have the last word. Let us love one another just as he loved us and we shall know the true life, that which does not die with death. To believe this does not make us enter into another world, some sort of Paradise; rather, it makes us live in another way, in a possible and meaningful world that Yeshua called the Kingdom of God. It is a world where Spirit, rather than competition and greed, reigns.

For some, the good news would take on more elaborate forms, according to the recollections of deeds and events that they studied, seeking to respond to the needs and questions of one or another community. Thus, the scribes who edited the gospels (without neglecting their own inspiration) remained in service to an authority that entrusted them with the task of putting elements of oral tradition into written form—useful for the development of a particular community. Here, we have not yet arrived at the stage of Church or institutionalization.

In this way, we can recognize the different communities and their special characteristics (and divergences) in the origins of the Gospels of John, Matthew, Luke, Mark, Thomas, Mary Magdalene, Philip, and so forth.

What might have been the nature of the community that produced the Gospel of Judas? What elements of oral tradition did the scribe select in composing this scripture? What authority, what movement, or what ideology was the scribe serving in putting together this text?

If it is true, as history suggests, that Judas was a Zealot, we might surmise that his gospel would be a collection emphasizing the words and deeds of Yeshua to correspond to those of a "Master of Justice." And we do find echoes of such words in the other gospels. In chapter 9 of this book, especially, but also in chapters 10 and 12, there is a suggestion of what might have been forms of words and behavior of Yeshua that would fit with this type of Messiah, whom the Zealots (but also many other disciples) believed they had found in Yeshua.

Thus, the Gospel of Judas would describe Yeshua's righteousness, seeing him as a kind of incarnation of the Torah, a man filled with enthusiasm for the Temple of YHWH, a Messiah who could rid the country of its Roman usurpers. Yet he would also restore peace, religious law, and justice in Israel; even more, he was a universal Messiah from the royal line of David, the one foretold by the prophets, who would establish the Kingdom of YHWH in all the lands of the earth after having established it in the Chosen Land.

Still another gospel of Judas is possible, inspired by a fervent and righteous disciple who loses faith in his Master-Messiah and in God. This gospel would be a narrative of a descent into hell, from which we return only after having burned all our inner and outer idols. This would be the narrative of an initiation, a Passover, a passage from the *me* to the I AM. A transformation of death orientation into orientation toward the One Who Is, beyond all opposites and antitheses, this other Judas gospel would also be an account of a death and resurrection, an echo of the death and resurrection experienced by Yeshua.

The recently discovered Gospel of Judas is something else. Though it remains one among many possible gospels of Judas, it is a Gnostic gospel.* Its existence was confirmed by St. Irenaeus, the first bishop of Lyon (Lugdanum), around the middle of the second century. Hence, the gospel itself has to be older than the mid-second century. The manuscript we now possess in fragments was copied sometime in the third century. It is a Sahidic Coptic translation of a Greek original and contains thirty-one folios of papyrus, or sixty-two pages. It was discovered in 1950 in Middle Egypt, at Muhazafat al-Minya. The codex containing the Gospel of Judas also contains two other apocrypha: the Epistle from Peter to Philip and the first Apocalypse of James.

What does this gospel say? Who were its sponsors? What ideas did it seek to promulgate? These are questions that have yet to be researched. For the present, let us recall what St. Irenaeus wrote in his *Adversus Haereses,* XXXI, c. 180:

> They claim that Judas the traitor knew much of these things, that Cain was the son of the supreme Power (the true God) and was a victim of the Creator (the false God, the bad Demiurge); and that Judas alone, a knower of truth like no other, had accomplished the mystery of betrayal; that through this act all things on earth and in heaven were shaken. They have produced a fictional history of this type, which they call the Gospel of Judas.

In this history, Judas appears as an instrument of the divine plan. "But all this has taken place so that the scriptures of the prophets might be fulfilled," say the canonical gospels. Judas is a necessary

---

*A good account of the vicissitudes surrounding this discovery is "Les tribulations d'un manuscrit apocryphe," published in the January 2006 issue of the French magazine *Science et Avenir.* [Generally, I try to avoid the widespread but confusing practice of capitalizing the word *gnostic,* but here the author is clearly referring to a certain current of theology, Christology, and philosophy of that era whose influence runs through many of the gnostic gospels—though it is notably absent in others, such as the gnostic (but not at all Gnostic) Gospel of Thomas. —*Trans.*]

actor for the revelation of the new Messiah—without him, there would have been no trial, no condemnation, no crucifixion, no resurrection, no Christianity.

Hence, for the Cainite-Judaite community, to which the Gospel of Judas belongs, the man Judas was a major player in the drama of salvation. In the same spirit that the Roman liturgy celebrates the *felix culpa,* the "happy fault," of original sin "which brought us such a Redeemer," the Cainite-Judaite liturgy celebrated the "happy betrayal which brought us such a Savior."

Contemporary authors such as Kazantzakis and Borges seem to have rediscovered this intuition. For Kazantzakis, it is Judas who helps Jesus fulfill a destiny that he had not the strength to accept alone; he is a sort of savior of the Savior. According to Borges, Judas helps Jesus grow to his full potential in choosing the most ignoble fault of denunciation: "It is as if he had been in exactly the same position as St. John the Baptist (the latter a holy man and not an accursed one—but holy for whom?). 'He must increase, but I must decrease.' (John 3:30) It is difficult to go further than this in the abnegation and denial of self."*

In any case, the outcome of Judas's act was the glorification of Yeshua, which recalls the Gospel of John (13:31):

> When Judas had left, Jesus said: "Now the Son of Man is glorified, and God has been glorified in him."

In this view, Judas participates in the glory of Yeshua and is as inseparable from him as night is from day.

In spite of the fact that they were quoted by a number of Church

*J. L. Borges, "Three Versions of Judas," in *Ficciones* (Baixa: Alianza Editorial, 1997). See also Michel Théron, *Petit lexique des hérésies chrétiennes* (Paris: Albin Michel, 2005), and Hyann Maccoby, *L'Exécuteur sacré* (Paris: Cerf, 1999).

fathers,* we know little about the Cainites or the Cainite-Judaites, the probable originators of the Gospel of Judas we now have. They recognized Cain as the son of a higher God than the God of Abel, identified as the bad Demiurge.

According to the Bible, it is Cain who has the idea of making an offering to God, and Abel only follows him (Genesis 4:3). For the Cainites, a God who preferred Abel's offering of a slaughtered lamb to an offering of the fruits of the earth could be only a false God, not only unjust (nowhere is it said that Cain was evil or had impure thoughts), but bloodthirsty as well.

Of course there are other ways of interpreting this passage from Genesis. For example, consider the meanings of the names Cain and Abel. Cain is the son who is everything to his mother: "I have acquired a man through YHWH,"† she says of her son, whence the name Qayin, from the Hebrew word *qanite,* "I acquired" or "I begot." (And what does she do with Adam?) Abel is only a sort of extension of his brother: "And again, she bore his brother Abel."‡ His Hebrew name, Hevel, signifies "nothing"—a breath of nothingness, mist.

It is too much for Cain to be everything to his mother and not enough for Abel to be nothing. Thus YHWH, by accepting the offering of Abel, the one who is nothing, may be seen as acting to restore a kind of justice. What can be added to someone is already everything?

This passage from Genesis has a later echo in the gospel parable of the master who sends his workers to the vineyard at different times.§ At the end of the day, the winegrower gives the workers who arrived at the last minute the same salary as those who arrived

---

*Irenaeus, *Adversus Haereses;* Epiphanius of Salamine, *Panarion;* Hippolytus, *Against Heresies,* 8; Pseudo-Tertullian, *Against All Heresies,* 7; Tertullian, *On Baptism*, 1.

†Genesis 4:1.

‡Genesis 4:2.

§Matthew 20.

earliest and worked long in the heat of the day. To Judas and some other disciples, it seemed like a flagrant injustice for the one who did practically nothing to receive as much as the one who did everything. But like YHWH, can Yeshua give other than what he had promised to one or the other? The conclusion of the text recalls the same attitude of YHWH toward Cain: "Must you be jealous because I am good?"

Perhaps the roots of Judas's jealousy and lack of understanding of Yeshua lie in his inability to accept this unconditional love for those who are nothing (in whose eyes?), as well as for those who are everything (again, in whose eyes?). Yet the gift of Being is more readily received by those who are nothing or who count for nothing.

Those who desire to be everything and all-powerful miss this grace and gratitude of Being. In their huge need to affirm their justice and their everything, are they not working toward annihilation of the Other? The "race of Cain," in this interpretation, means a race of violent people that would include Judas. Yeshua, on the other hand, in his nonaction, would belong to the race of Abel (the victims, the weak, the good-for-nothings) and would bear witness to another kind of justice.

This reading of Genesis would, of course, disagree with that of the Cainites and their Gospel of Judas. They prefer a gnostic interpretation—which should not be confused with Gnostic (from *gnosis*).*

Faced with the overwhelming amount of injustice, bloodshed, and suffering that pervades this world, the Cainites, like other Gnostics, could not imagine that such a creation could be the work of a good God. Therefore, there must be another God higher than the one the Bible says created all this. This is the true God, the one whom Cain honored with his vegetarian offerings. This deity goes by other names as well: the Unknown God and the Allogene, for

*See my studies on the multiple meanings of the term *gnosis* in Jean-Yves Leloup, *Introduction aux vrais philosophes* (Paris: Albin Michel, 1998). [See also the note on page 151. —*Trans.*]

example. In the Gospel of Judas, Yeshua himself bears the name of the Allogene (meaning "stranger"). This name is also applied to Seth, the third son of Adam and Eve.

This is not the place for a full and exhaustive exegesis of the Gospel of Judas, but an interesting question comes immediately to mind: Does not the relationship between Cain and Abel prefigure the relationship between Judas and Yeshua? Some scholars have even hypothesized a literal kinship relation in the latter: Like James, Judas may have been an actual brother of Yeshua.*

We must also take into account the fact that the document published by the National Geographic Society is very incomplete. A good half of the gospel is missing. As in similar cases, this very gap in the text forces us to rediscover our freedom of imagination—though of course limited by what we do know from other texts from the Nag Hammadi library.

Most of them present us with a Yeshua who is *allogene,* entirely Other, and unknown for many. This is no doubt a Gnostic figure, one who "knows" what he is doing and shares this knowledge with Judas. This should give us pause to reflect on a saying that has sometimes been removed from our recent Bible but was found in older versions:†

Having seen a man working on the day of Shabbat, Yeshua said to him: "Man, you are happy if you know what you are doing. If you do not know, you are miserable, for you are transgressing the Law."

To transgress the law in full consciousness of what we do is thus a minor fault in comparison to remaining unconscious.

Did not Yeshua tell Judas, "You know what you must do, so do it quickly"? Be conscious and do what you can. The only real fault is to remain unconscious, asleep, intoxicated (refer to *The Gospel of*

---

*See Pierre-Antoine Bernheim, *Jacques, frère de Jésus* (Paris: Albin Michel, 1996).

†See the Bezan Codex, Luke 6:4. [The Bezan Codex is one of the oldest Christian scripture manuscripts, dating from the sixth century. —*Trans.*]

*Truth,* Jung Codex). The only salvation is in abiding in wakefulness. The Jesus who emerges from the Nag Hammadi scriptures is more than the Master of justice revered by the Zealots and the authors of the Dead Sea Scrolls. He is a Master of wisdom who initiates mortal human beings into their uncreated, eternal life.

But access to this ever-present truth, which is also the true nature of human beingness, requires passing through a certain number of trials. These are passages into temple spaces or climates, which constitute the intermediary worlds of the soul *(psyche)* inhabited by the innumerable memories of our terrestrial life. The soul must undergo various purifications or sacrifices before it can contemplate the pure light. Yeshua is the guide, both earthly and otherworldly, in this adventure. He is the One who helps us to create the bridge between these different worlds.*

The Gospel of Judas presents Judas as Yeshua's favorite disciple, the great initiate and the leader of a church or community of all the Cainites. This doubtless makes it of limited interest, but it puts an interesting spotlight on the figure of Judas:

> They came back to Judas and told him: "Even if you feel
> wrong in this role, you are the true disciple of Yeshua."†

In the creation of this gospel, we can detect a process that also characterizes the redactions of the canonical and pseudepigraphical gospels: The text is edited by a community of witnesses or believers, all of whom invoke the authority of a major figure. This figure is usually presented as the appointed leader, the favorite disciple

---

*See Jean-Yves Leloup, *The Gospel of Mary Magdalene* (Rochester, Vt.: Inner Traditions, 2002).

†*Evangile de Judas,* translation by Charles W. Hedrick. [This passage does not occur in the *National Geographic* translation. For more information on the work of Hedrick and on this gospel, see www.earlychristianwritings.com/gospeljudas.html. —*Trans.*]

or someone who was the intimate friend—even the twin—of the Teacher himself. For the community of Mark, this figure was Simon, head of the apostles. For the Johannine community, it was John, "the disciple Jesus loved." In the Gospel of Thomas, this person was Thomas, called Didymus, which means "twin." In the Gospel of Mary Magdalene, it is Miriam, the intimate companion of Yeshua who transmits words of truth. In the Gospel of Judas, the major initiate is of course Judas, whose mission is to "deliver" *(paredosis)* Yeshua and reveal his light to the world.

No one knows what Yeshua really said. All we know is what others heard and what they chose to remember from all they heard—a process no doubt influenced by what comforted them most in their own convictions or opinions. The Gospel of Judas, like that of John, Matthew, or Miriam, is not the "gospel truth," but rather a record of a certain way of seeing the world, a certain way of listening, understanding, and loving the Teacher.

The figure of Yeshua thus remains a multifaceted diamond whose totality none can grasp. In spite of their divergences, the gospels are not opposed but are instead complementary. The views of Judas, Miriam, Yohanan, and Matthew form an ensemble that witnesses to the same presence of Yeshua—infinitely close, yet ungraspable. How many more gospels would be needed to reveal the full brilliance of this diamond?

## *A Russian Novel?*

While writing a screenplay, Michelle de Broca, Patrick Alessandrin, and Natasha Alessandrin asked me questions, mostly historical, about Judas. I wrote the first chapters of my narrative in an attempt to synthesize, in an accessible form, a large body of documents and studies, sometimes fascinating but often boring and almost always contradicting each other.

Then I abandoned this effort of historical reconstruction in favor of the discovery of the archetypal wealth revealed in the figure of Judas. His complexity fascinated me, and it was during my effort to enter into his psychology that I discovered my kinship with two Russians: first, Leonid Andreyev (his novel *Judas Iscariot and Others*), and then a rediscovery of Dostoyevsky and *The Brothers Karamazov.* Andreyev's references to the latter in his last chapters are almost as explicit as his gospel quotations.

The experience of doubt, revolt, the shadow, the descent into hell, and the question of freedom now appeared to me as eminently contemporary themes that had already been explored, at least partially, by Dostoyevsky's characters.

Sometimes it seems that Dostoyevsky was attempting to write the biography of a great sinner—his last novels would seem to be fragments of this larger story. Paul Evdokimov points out that the word *jitye,* used by Dostoyevsky, is traditionally used in the Russian Orthodox Church to designate the life of a saint, a life oriented toward God. And thus it remains for this novelist, even when the life is one of struggle and revolt against God.

This is the revolt of Ivan in *The Brothers Karamazov:* "If God exists, then life on earth must be the Kingdom of God, where all is clarity and measure; on the other hand, if the world is one of riddles and contradictions, repugnant to reason, then God does not exist."

Like Judas, Ivan seems to be a kind of Job who has definitively chosen rebellion. For Ivan, the irrational can be only absurd. Not content to return his ticket to God as a protest against the disastrous absurdity of creation, he feels obliged to repudiate all transcendence.*

The European nihilism of Ivan, like the universal nihilism of Judas, reminds us of the potential of human freedom to deny Being

---

*Refer to Olivier Clément's introduction to Paul Evdokimov, *Dostoïevski et le problème du mal* (Bilbao: Desclée de Brouwer, 1979), viii–ix.

and to use this potential of negation to conceive a sort of objective Nothingness that swallows and annihilates everything. This nihilism can be overcome only by an unexpected, irrational experience—one that brings grace (transcendence) this time, rather than the usual absurdity. This is the experience of death and resurrection of which Dostoyevsky and certain of his characters had a premonition. It is the experience of Judas, the man betrayed by his ideal Messiah—as well as that of Job, betrayed by his good God.

In certain chapters of this book I have attempted to give a hint of the shadow of Dostoyevsky's Grand Inquisitor, especially in the chapter of the encounter between Yeshua and Judas in the desert. I do not come to the same conclusions that Dostoyevsky did, however. Most of us are familiar with the famous passage from *Crime and Punishment* in which the Inquisitor—who represents the power of reason, justice, and a happiness to be imposed upon all—seems to be condemned by the compassion incarnated by Christ:

> In the Last Judgment, He will say: "Come, you others, you too come to me! Come, you drunks, you shameless ones!" And we shall all go forward with no shame . . . and He will say: "You pigs, your image is that of the beast, and you bear his stamp: but come to me, nevertheless." And then the sages, the men of reason, will cry: "Lord, how can you also accept them?" And He will reply: "O sages, O men of reason, if I accept them, it is because not a single one of them has ever judged himself worthy of the Beyond." And He will open his arms to us, and we will fall into his embrace, and weep . . . and we will understand everything . . .

But our task is to go still further, for compassion cannot condemn justice. The reality beyond must contain both compassion and justice as well as welcoming for the Grand Inquisitor himself and all those who do not want to be welcomed in their refusal of God and of Being, for this refusal of Being, or God, is still a manifestation of Being, just as the refusal of intelligence sometimes called *agnosticism* is a manifestation of intelligence *(gnosis).*

The question raised by my narrative of Judas is not only "Cain, what have you done to your brother?" It is also "Abel, what have you done to your brother?" It is not only "Judas, what have you done to Yeshua?" It is also "Yeshua, what have you done to Judas?"

This is where it ceases to be a historical novel or a "Russian" novel to become an Orthodox writing evoking the early Christian faith in this *apocatastasis* in which all will be saved, "even the damned, and even the demons." This must not be construed as a rationale for a permissiveness where everything is allowed, but rather as an invitation to a life delivered of guilt and fear, where all is but order and chaos, kindness and violence, delight and bitterness.

The surrender to *what is* is the first step toward that sense which overflows from all our rationalities (the binary functioning of our brain) and is the fulfillment of a paradoxical real:

The One who was . . . who is . . . who is coming . . .

# Appendix B

## *Gospel References*

In addition to the texts concerning Judas, I have included the story of the adulteress and the story of the temptation in the desert, two key moments in the narrative of the divergence between Judas and Yeshua.*

### *Judas, One of the Twelve*

*Matthew 10:1–4*

> And he called to him his twelve disciples and gave them power over unclean spirits, to cast them out, and to heal every disease and every infirmity.
>
> The names of the twelve apostles are the following:
> First, Simon, called Peter;
> Andrew his brother;
> James the son of Zebedee;

*[The following gospel quotations are English translations of the author's own French translations from the Greek. —*Trans.*]

John his brother;
Philip and Bartholomew; Thomas;
Matthew the publican;
James the son of Alphaeus;
Thaddaeus;
Simon the Zealot;
and Judas Iscariot,
the same one who delivered him.

*Mark 3:13–19*

Yeshua climbed the mountain. He called to him those whom he wanted. They came to him, and he appointed twelve to be with him, and to be sent out to preach and have authority to cast out demons. He appointed Simon and gave him the name of Peter; then James the son of Zebedee and John the brother of James, whom he surnamed Boanerges, that is, sons of thunder; Andrew; and Philip; and Bartholomew; and Matthew; and Thomas; and James, the son of Alphaeus; and Thaddaeus; and Simon the Cananaean; and Judas Iscariot, the same one who delivered him.

*Luke 6:13–16*

Yeshua spent the night praying to God. And when it was morning, he called his disciples [*matetes*], and chose from them twelve, whom he named apostles [*apostolos*]: Simon, whom he named Peter, and Andrew his brother, and James and John, and Philip, and Bartholomew, and Matthew, and Thomas, and James the son of Alphaeus, and Simon who was called the Zealot, and Judas the son of James, and Judas Iscariot, who became a traitor [*egeneto prodotes*]. (See also John 1:14, *Kai o logos sarx egeneto.*)

*John 6:63–71*

"It is the spirit [*pneuma*] that gives life; the flesh [*sarx*] is not necessary. The words that I have spoken to you are breath [*pneuma*] and life [*zoe*]. But there are some of you that do not subscribe [*pisteousin*]." For Jesus knew from the first who those were that did not subscribe, and who it was that would deliver him [*paradoson*]. And he said, "This is why I tell you that no one can come to me unless it is given to him by the Father . . ."

. . . "Did I not choose you, the twelve? Among you, there is a devil [*diabolon*]." He spoke of Judas the son of Simon, the Iscariot, the one who was to deliver him [*para didonai*]; him, one of the twelve.

## *The Scene at Bethany*

*John 12:1–8*

Six days before the Passover, Yeshua came to Bethany, where Lazarus was, whom Jesus had raised from the dead [*ou egeiren ek nekron*].

There they made a supper in his honor: Martha served, and Lazarus was one of those at table with him. Mary took a pound of costly ointment of pure nard and anointed [*eleifen*] the feet of Jesus and wiped his feet with her hair; and the house was filled with the fragrance of the ointment. But Judas Iscariot, one of his disciples, he who was to deliver him, said, "Why was this ointment not sold for three hundred denarii and given to the poor?" This he said, not that he cared for the poor but because he was a thief, and as it was he who kept the money box, he used to take away what was put into it.

Jesus then said, "Leave her be! Let her keep it for the day of my burial. The poor you will always have with you, but you will not always have me."

*Mark 14:3–10*

Yeshua was at Bethany in the house of Simon the leper. As he sat at table, a woman came with an alabaster flask of ointment of pure nard, very costly, and she broke the flask and poured it over his head. But there were some who said to each other indignantly, "Why was the ointment thus wasted? For this ointment might have been sold for more than three hundred denarii, and given to the poor." And they reproached her. But Jesus said, "Let her alone; why do you trouble her? What she has accomplished for me is a beautiful thing. For you always have the poor with you, and whenever you will, you can do good to them; but you will not always have me. She has done what she could; she has anointed my body beforehand for burying. And truly [*amen*], I say to you, wherever the gospel is preached in the whole world, what she has done will be told in memory of her." Then Judas Iscariot, who was one of the twelve, went to the high priests in order to deliver Yeshua, and said: "What will you give me if I deliver him to you?" And they paid him thirty pieces of silver [*arguria*].

*Matthew 26:6–15*

Now when Jesus was at Bethany in the house of Simon the leper, a woman came up to him with an alabaster flask of very expensive ointment, and she poured it on his head as he sat at table. But when the disciples saw it, they were indignant, saying, "Why this waste? For this ointment might have been sold for a large sum, and given to the poor." But Jesus, aware of this, said to them, "Why do you trouble the woman? For she has done a beautiful thing to me. For you always have the poor with you, but you will not always have me. In pouring this ointment on my body she has done it to prepare me for burial. Truly, I say to you, wherever this gospel is preached in the whole world, what she has done will be told in memory of her." Then one of the twelve, who was called Judas Iscariot, went to the chief priests and said, "What will you give me if I deliver him to you?" And they paid him thirty pieces of silver.

## *The Washing of the Feet*

*John 13:1–5*

Before the feast of the Passover, when Yeshua knew that his hour had come to depart out of this world to the Father, having loved his own who were in the world, he loved them to the end [*telos*]. And during supper, when the devil [*diabolon*] had already put it into the heart of Judas Iscariot, Simon's son, to betray him, Yeshua, knowing that the Father had given all things into His hands, and that he had come from God and was going to God [*theon*], rose from the table, laid aside his garments, and girded himself with a towel. Then he poured water into a basin, and began to wash the disciples' feet, and to wipe them with the towel with which he was girded.

*John 13:10–11*

Yeshua said to Peter: "He who has bathed does not need to wash, for he is entirely pure [*katharos*] and you are pure, but not all of you." For he knew who was to deliver him; that was why he said, "You are not all pure."

*John 13:12–16*

When he had washed their feet, Yeshua took his garments, resumed his place at table, and said to them, "Do you know what I have done for you? You call me Master and Lord; and you are right, for so I am [*eimi*]. If I, your Lord and Master, have washed your feet, you also ought to wash one another's feet. For I have given you an example, that you also should do as I have done to you. Truly, truly, I say to you [*amen, amen, lego*], a servant is not greater than his master . . . "

## *The Last Supper*

*Matthew 26:20–25*

When it was evening, he sat at table with the twelve disciples, and as they were eating, he said, "Truly, I say to you, one of you will deliver me." And they were very sorrowful, and began to say to him one after another, "Could it be I, Lord?" He answered, "He who has dipped his hand in the dish with me, will deliver me. The Son of Man departs as it is written of him, but woe to that man by whom the Son of man is delivered! It would have been better for that man if he had not been born." Judas, who delivered him, spoke, saying: "Could it be I, Master?" He replied to him, "You have said it!"

*Luke 22:21–23*

"Behold: The hand of him who delivers me is on this table. For the Son of Man departs as it has been determined; but woe to that man by whom he is delivered!" And they began to question one another, which of them it was that would do this.

*Mark 14:17–21*

As they were at table eating, Yeshua said, "Truly, I say to you, one of you will deliver me, one who is eating with me." They began to be sorrowful, and to say to him one after another, "Could it be I?" He said to them, "It is one of the twelve, one who dips his hand into the same dish with me. For the Son of Man departs as it is written of him, but woe [*ouai*] to that man [*anthropos*] by whom the Son of Man [*anthropon*] is delivered! It would have been better for that man if he had not been born [*egenete*]."

*John 13:17–32*

"I know those whom I have chosen; it is that the scripture may be fulfilled: 'He who ate bread with me has lifted his heel against me.' I tell you this now, before it happens, that when it does happen, you may believe that I AM [*ego eimi; I am that I am*]. Amen, amen, I say to you, he who receives anyone whom I send receives me; and he who receives me, receives Him who sent me."

When Yeshua had thus spoken, he was troubled in his mind, and solemnly declared, "Truly, truly, I say to you, one of you will deliver me."

The disciples looked at one another, uncertain of whom he spoke. One of his disciples, whom Yeshua loved [*agapē*], was lying close to the breast [*kolpo*] of Yeshua; so Simon Peter beckoned to him and said, "Tell us who it is of whom he speaks."

So leaning close to Yeshua, he asked him, "Lord, who is it?"

Yeshua answered, "It is he to whom I shall give this morsel when I have dipped it." So when he had dipped the morsel, he gave it to Judas, the son of Simon Iscariot.

As soon as he had received the morsel, Satan [Satanas] entered into him. Yeshua said to him, "What you have to do, do it quickly [*poeson takion*]."

No one at the table knew why he said this to him.

Some thought that because Judas kept the money purse, Yeshua was telling him to buy something needed for the feast, or perhaps that he should give something to the poor. After receiving the morsel, Judas immediately left. It was night.

When he had gone, Yeshua said, "Now the Son of man has been glorified [*doxasei*], and through him God is glorified. God will glorify him in himself, and He will glorify him soon."

## *The Delivery and Its Price*

*Matthew 26:14–16 and Mark 14:10–11*

Judas Iscariot, one of the twelve, went to the high priests to deliver Yeshua to them. They rejoiced at this news, and promised to give him silver, and Judas sought as to how he would deliver him at the right moment.

*Luke 22:1–6*

Now the feast of Unleavened Bread known as Passover drew near. The chief priests and the scribes were seeking how to put Yeshua to death; for they feared the people. Then Satan [Shatan] entered into Judas called Iscariot, who was one of the twelve. Judas went to speak with the chief priests and officers of the guards, as to how he might deliver him to them. They were very glad, and promised to give him money. Judas agreed, and sought an opportunity to deliver him to them without the knowledge of the crowd.

## *Yeshua's Arrest*

*Matthew 26:47–50*

While he was still speaking, Judas, one of the twelve, came. He brought with him a large troop armed with swords and clubs, from the chief priests and the elders of the people. Now his deliverer had given them a sign, saying, "The one I shall kiss is the man; arrest him."

Then he came up to Jesus at once and said, "Hail, Rabbi!" [*kaire, Rabbi; Rejoice, Rabbi!*] And he gave him a kiss [*katephilesen*]. Jesus said to him, "My friend, this is why you are here [*ephoparei*]."

*Mark 14:43–46*

And while Yeshua was still speaking, Judas came, one of the twelve, and with him a troop armed with swords and clubs, sent by the high priests, the scribes, and the elders. Now the deliverer had given them a sign, saying, "The one I shall embrace [*philyso*] is the man; seize him and lead him away well guarded."

As soon as he arrived, he went up to him at once, and said, "Rabbi!" And he kissed him [*katephilesen*]. And they laid hands on him and arrested him.

*Luke 22:47–53*

Yeshua was still speaking when a crowd appeared. Judas, one of the twelve, was leading it. He approached Yeshua to embrace him [*philesai*]. Yeshua said to him: "Judas, it is by a kiss [*philemati*] that you deliver the Son of Man."

*John 18:2–12*

When Yeshua had spoken these words, he went forth with his disciples across the Kidron valley, where there was a garden, which he and his disciples entered. Now Judas, who delivered him, also knew the place; for Yeshua often went there with his disciples. So Judas, leading a band of soldiers and some officers from the chief priests and the Pharisees, went there with lanterns and torches and weapons. Then Yeshua, knowing all that was to befall him, came forward and said to them, "Whom do you seek?"

They answered him, "Yeshua of Nazareth." Yeshua said to them, "I am he" [*ego eimi*]. Judas, who betrayed him, was standing with them. When he said to them, "I am he," they drew back and fell to the ground. Again he asked them, "Whom do you seek?" And they said, "Yeshua of Nazareth." Yeshua answered, "I told you that it is I; so, if you seek me, let these men go." This was to fulfill the word that he had spoken, "Of those whom you gave to me I lost not one."

Then Simon Peter, who wore a sword, drew it and struck the high priest's slave and cut off his right ear. The slave's name was Malchus.

But Yeshua said to Peter, "Put your sword into its sheath! Shall I not drink the cup that the Father has given me?"

## *The Death of Judas*

*Matthew 27:1–10*

When morning came, all the chief priests and the elders of the people took counsel against Yeshua to put him to death; and they bound him and led him away and delivered him to Pilate, the governor.

When Judas, who had delivered him, saw that he was condemned, he returned to himself [*metameletheis: meta* means "going beyond"; *lethe* means "forgetfulness"] and gave back the thirty pieces of silver to the chief priests and the elders, saying, "I have sinned in betraying innocent blood." They said, "Why turn back against us? Deal with it yourself."

Then he threw down the pieces of silver in the temple, and he went and hanged himself [*apegazato*].

But the chief priests, taking the pieces of silver, said, "It is not permitted to put it into the treasury, since it is blood money."

So they took counsel, and used it to buy the potter's field, to bury strangers in. Therefore that field has been called the Field of Blood to this day.

Then was fulfilled what had been spoken by the prophet Jeremiah, saying, "And they took the thirty pieces of silver. It was the price of him on whom a price had been set by some of the sons of Israel. And they gave them for the potter's field, as the Lord had commanded me."

### *Acts 1:15–25*

Peter stood up among the brethren (the company of persons was in all about a hundred and twenty), and said, "My brothers, the scripture had to be fulfilled, which the Holy Spirit spoke previously through the mouth of David, concerning Judas who became guide to those who arrested Yeshua.

"For he was one of ours, and was allotted his share [*diakonias*] in this ministry. Then this man bought a field with the salary [*misthou*] of his injustice [*adikias*]. There, he fell headlong, and burst open in the middle and all his bowels gushed out. This became known to all the inhabitants of Jerusalem, so that the field was called in their language Hakeldaima, that is, Field of Blood. This is what was written in the book of Psalms: 'Let his home become empty, and let no one to live there and then, let another take charge of it . . . '"

. . . And they prayed and said, "You, Lord, who know the hearts of all, show which one of these two thou hast chosen to take the place in this ministry and apostleship which Judas abandoned, to go to his own place."

And they cast lots, and the lot fell on Matthias; and he was enrolled with the eleven apostles.

## *The Adulteress*

*John 8:1–11*

Yeshua went to the Mount of Olives. But at dawn, he was again within the walls of the temple; all the people came to him, and he sat down and taught them.

The *sopherim** and the Pharisees brought a woman who had been caught in the act of adultery. They made her stand before everyone, and said to Yeshua: "Rabbi, this woman has been caught in the act of adultery. In the Torah, Moshe has commanded us to stone such women. What do you say about her?" They were saying this to test him, that they might have a reason to accuse him.

Yeshua leaned down and wrote with his finger on the ground. And since they continued to ask him, he stood up and said to them: "Let whoever is without sin cast the first stone at her." And once more he bent down and wrote with his finger on the ground.

---

**Sopherim* (Hebrew), *grammatos* (Greek), and *scribae* (Latin) all refer to literati, scholars of scripture, theologians—that is, scribes.

When they heard these words, they went away, one by one, beginning with the eldest.

Yeshua was left alone with the woman. Standing up, he said to her, "Woman, where are they? Has no one condemned you?"

She said, "No one, Lord." And Yeshua said, "Neither do I condemn you. Go, and sin no more."

## *The Temptation in the Desert*

*Luke 4:1–13*

And Yeshua, after having been plunged in the waters of the Jordan by Yohanan the Baptist, was led by the Holy Spirit to the wilderness. There, he was tested by the devil for forty days. He ate nothing during those days. He was hungry.

The devil then said to him, "If you are the Son of God [*iou tou theou*], transform this stone into food [*arto*]."

And Yeshua answered him, "It is written, 'Man does not live by bread alone.'"

And the devil lifted him on high, and showed him all the kingdoms of the world, and said to him: "I will give you the glory and the power of all these nations; for they are mine, and I give their riches to whom I will. If you will prostrate yourself before me [*proskuneses*], the entire world shall be yours."

Yeshua answered him, "It is written, 'You shall prostrate yourself only in the Presence of the One Who Is (YHWH), and Him only shall you worship.'"

Then the devil took him to Jerusalem, and set him on the pinnacle of the temple, and said to him, "If you are the Son of God, throw yourself down from here; for it is written, 'He will order his angels protect you, and they will bear you in their hands, lest you hurt your foot on a stone.'"

And Yeshua answered him, "It is said, 'You shall not tempt the Lord your God.'"

Having exhausted all forms of temptation, the devil departed from him, waiting for a favorable occasion [*kairos*].

## *Books of Related Interest*

THE SACRED EMBRACE OF JESUS AND MARY
*The Sexual Mystery at the Heart of the Christian Tradition*
by Jean-Yves Leloup

THE GOSPEL OF MARY MAGDALENE
by Jean-Yves Leloup
Foreword by Jacob Needleman

THE GOSPEL OF THOMAS
*The Gnostic Wisdom of Jesus*
by Jean-Yves Leloup
Foreword by Jacob Needleman

THE GOSPEL OF PHILIP
*Jesus, Mary Magdalene, and the Gnosis of Sacred Union*
by Jean-Yves Leloup
Foreword by Jacob Needleman

JESUS AFTER THE CRUCIFIXION
*From Jerusalem to Rennes-le-Château*
by Graham Simmans

THE WOMAN WITH THE ALABASTER JAR
*Mary Magdalen and the Holy Grail*
by Margaret Starbird

THE DISCOVERY OF THE NAG HAMMADI TEXTS
*A Firsthand Account of the Expedition That Shook the Foundations of Christianity*
by Jean Doresse

FORBIDDEN RELIGION
*Suppressed Heresies of the West*
Edited by J. Douglas Kenyon